Christopher Heller

Infant Baptism
BASICS

The Pastoral Press
Washington, DC

"Babies Learn Sounds of Language by Six Months," by Sandra Blakeslee, *New York Times*, February 4, 1992; copyright © 1992 by The New York Times Company. Reprinted by permission.

Excerpts from *Christian Initiation: General Introduction*, copyright 1985, International Commission on English in the Liturgy; excerpts from the *Rite of Baptism for Children*, copyright 1969, International Commission on English in the Liturgy.

Logos by Rev. Bill Hanson.

ISBN 1-56929-013-X

Copyright © The Pastoral Press, 1993
All Rights Reserved

The Pastoral Press
225 Sheridan Street, N.W.
Washington, D.C. 20011
(202) 723-1254

The Pastoral Press is the publications division of the National Association of Pastoral Musicians, a membership organization of musicians and clergy dedicated to fostering the art of musical liturgy.

Printed in the United States of America

Contents

Foreword 1
Introduction 5

Shaping a Vision 9
Going Public 13
Extending Personal Invitations 17
The Informational Meeting 19

Sponsor Formation: Introduction 27
Sponsor Formation: Session One 29
Sponsor Formation: Session Two 33
Sponsor Formation: Session Three 51

The Welcoming Session 61
The Gathering Session 63
The Baptismal Celebration 71
The Reflection/Follow-Up Session

The Past and the Future 81

Appendices
 1. Sample Homily 89
 2. Outline of the Process (For Sponsors) 92
 3. Target Letter to Interested Persons 94
 4. Psalms of Praise 96
 5. Contents of Packet for Sponsors 99
 6. Contents of Packet for Parents 100
 7. Contents of Packet for Director/Facilitator 101
 8. Ice Breaker Questions 102
 9. Summary of Doctrinal Updates 104

10. Data Sheet on Baptism 106
11. Welcome Cover Letter to Sponsors 109
12. Welcome Letter to Couples with New Babies 111
13. Outline of the Process (For Parents) 112
14. "If Children . . ." 114
15. The Sign of the Cross 115
16. Parish Skills Survey 116
17. "If Men Got Pregnant" 118
18. Saints for Boys and Girls 119
19. Reminders for Baptism 127
20. Parents' Prayer after Their Child's Baptism 129
21. Babies Learn Sounds of Language 130
22. Parent Evaluation Sheet 133
23. Parish Sponsor Evaluation Sheet 134
24. Reminder Letter to Parents 136
25. Invitation to a Reunion Mass 137
26. Listening Skills 138

Foreword

In June 1990, my partner Father Bill Hanson and I were assigned as co-pastors of St. Gerard Majella in Port Jefferson Station, New York. Our parish community is located on Long Island, in the "suburbs" east of New York City. Soon approaching its twenty-fifth anniversary, St. Gerard's parish community has enjoyed the reputation of reaching out to persons in need, particularly those requiring our quick and immediate action. Aware of this tradition and reputation, the people of the parish also wanted to expand their concern beyond crisis interventions to everyday experiences. In September 1990 we held open listening sessions, to which we invited all parishioners, to help us understand the roots of the parish as well as to forge a vision. We believed (and we still do!) that it is important to consult with parishioners regarding the past as well as the future. One of the priorities voiced at all the listening sessions, and verified in a survey conducted during weekend eucharists, was the need for ways to meet new people in the parish and to greet newcomers with a true spirit of hospitality.

It also quickly became clear to us and to the parish pastoral staff that two full-time priests could not adequately begin to address the needs of almost four thousand families on a regular basis. We had already begun to explore models for restructuring parishes and re-imagining what the church as the people of God could look like as we move toward the twenty-first century. The vision of Father Art Baranowski made the most sense to us. Rather than simply add another program to an already hectic parish schedule, Baranowski

Art Baranowski entitles his process *Called to be Church*, and it is explained in his book *Creating Small Faith Communities: A Plan for Restructuring Your Parish and Renewing Catholic Life*. Cincinnati, OH: St. Anthony Messenger Press, 1988.

helped us to step back and reflect on ways in which we could more effectively help our parishioners *become* church for one another. In his own humble but powerful way, he also empowered us with a reality check: we needed to realize that we could *not* be or do all things for all people. We needed to formulate a modest proposal and action plan.

Once we had accepted the premise that we would not function as a parish of programs but would instead work to form small Christian communities within the parish faith community, we began to apply that vision to individual circumstances and already existing programs and groups. High on the list of things to examine were two other parishioner priorities gleaned from the survey and our listening sessions. These were:

• the importance of life-giving liturgical celebrations and opportunities to pray and grow spiritually; and

• the crucial role of religious education and other programs of faith formation.

In light of these issues, it was natural and not at all surprising that we chose to look at infant baptism in all its aspects: remote and proximate preparation, an invitation to catechesis and the challenge that the sacramental rite offers, the celebration of the word and movement to the font, a follow-up session, and the pastoral issues that arise in each stage of the process.

What follows is one evolving experience of one parish's response to the experience of infant baptism. This book is for directors of parish infant baptism programs and for those faithful ministers who will work with them to become the hands and legs of Christ Jesus. Naturally, some of the circumstances will not apply directly to each person's faith community or life situation. What this step-by-step process does offer, however, is a basic, tried, and successful infant baptism process which emphasizes the ecclesial or communal-church dimension rather than the privatized situation experienced by many of us in the past. Not only is the Sunday assembly included in the welcoming and initiating of infants into the church, but our parishioners now expect to sing the appropriate accompanying acclamations during baptisms at eucharist and are ready to do so.

The goals of recent church documents such as *Music in Catholic Worship* and *Liturgical Music Today*, which specify full conscious and active participation as our task, continue to inspire us.

Obviously, the challenge of looking critically at an already-existing parish program for infant baptism cannot be shouldered by a single person. Our parish has been able to accomplish much in a short time span because of God's grace and by using the talents and gifts of many persons with whom we minister. In addition to our other co-pastor Father Bill Hanson, there are the various members of our parish staff, all of whom continue to function as the "brain trust" for the process. There is also a large group of persons who are "bridges" for those who seek the fullness of life for those entrusted to their care. We have chosen to call these persons our parish sponsors. They personally and generously reach out to welcome those who wish to present their children for baptism. We are personally and particularly grateful to those who were part of our "first wave," who came to an information meeting and several training sessions. They brought their enthusiasm, their love for God and the church, and their encouragement when this process existed in seedling form.

Thanks also to the various parishes in the Diocese of Rockville Centre who expressed interest in our approach, and to the Diocesan Offices of Catechesis and Worship and Pastoral Formation, who early in our formulations afforded us opportunities to present the vision and gather feedback on the process.

Foreword

Introduction

Old Horizons and New, The Way We Were and Are: The Birth of a New Vision

Catechists and liturgists alike have known for years that many of our parish programs preparing families and godparents to celebrate the baptism of infants fail in many ways. Other than parishes offering no sessions or assistance toward sacramental readiness (failures in their own right), the following composite scenario may typify or indicate reasons to explain our past lack of success:

- the parent making the initial contact is told in matter-of-fact language about the parish's policy for infant baptism; the secretary who repeats this information many times each month in the same monotone voice offers no greeting or congratulations to this generally-unchurched potential parishioner-caller;
- couples and individuals arrive upon church property with no familiarity of buildings or specific locations, and no persons or signs to direct them to their destination;
- the room in which sessions are held is poorly lighted; the chairs are uncomfortable; and no refreshments are in sight;
- some registration material or printed information may be distributed, but there are no personal introductions to the other persons attending, nor are name-tags provided;
- the presence of infants is tolerated as a necessary evil, brought on by the shortage of baby-sitters or the economic crunch or both, but it is not encouraged;

"The preparation for baptism and Christian instruction are both of vital concern to God's people, the Church, which hands on and nourishes the faith received from the apostles" (*Christian Initiation: General Introduction* 7).

"... it is most important that catechists and other laypersons should work with priests and deacons in the preparation for baptism" (*Christian Initiation: General Introduction* 7).

- the meeting opens with a perfunctory prayer which is framed by two hastily-made signs of the cross;
- the lay or religious or clergy coordinator begins what is essentially a forty-five minute monologue on the history, theology, and the liturgy of baptism; he or she speaks in a classroom lecture style, a style most find quite boring;
- significant time and attention are devoted to limbo, original sin and purgatory, without providing an understanding that links secondary theology (the doctrines and teachings) to primary-level theology (the lived experience which gives birth to those teachings);
- dates and times for baptism are announced and final questions are answered;
- as Shakespeare wrote, *all exit*.

One might experience a profound despair or sadness based on what is contained or omitted in the above description. However, admitting our failures and declaring our willingness to search for preferred alternatives is a first and positive step in ameliorating the situation. By suggesting that a program of baptismal preparation should be informed and influenced by the Rite of Christian Initiation of Adults (RCIA), we simply recognize several needs (among others) at once:

- the need for conscious connections among the many ways a person is initiated into the church;
- the need to integrate into a parish's lived experience a contemporary understanding of baptism as a paschal event;
- the need to call Christian women and men to accountability as parish sponsors and welcomers of new members.

A NEW APPROACH

Our approach, however:

- invites each parish community to "look inward before looking and reaching out";

Introduction

- divides infant baptism into a four-part process, noting the personnel, content, and ritual moments of each part;
- summarizes the plan and notes some concerns or challenges we anticipated in the
    —transition between programs and
    —in the necessary catechesis of the assembly;
- comments on the first evaluation process after beginning this program;
- offers a prognosis for the future.

"In order to enliven . . . faith, the Church prescribes . . . the preparation of the children's parents . . ." (*Christian Initiation: General Introduction* 3).

SOME VOCABULARY

Before explaining all this we want to clarify some vocabulary that we will use.

• The term "Sunday Masses" also recognizes the existence of one or more Saturday evening vigil Masses. We emphasize Sunday because of its central place in the development of the liturgical year; Sunday is the first day of the week, the eighth day of a new creation, and the Lord's Day. Sunday summarizes the paschal mystery of God's love for us in Christ, and of persons becoming the People of God in communal settings.

• The word "parish" is used because the parish is the place where most persons experience and participate in the sacred mysteries and in the church's sacramental life. There are in fact Catholic communities that gather regularly for worship in other settings.

• The term "church building" refers to the place where the community's meeting rooms are located. It is here that the large-group sessions will be held. In some places, this facility is called the parish center, or community house, or parish school. We want to use the term "church" primarily to refer to the *people* rather than a place.

• "Pastoral staff" is a generic term for the leadership core group of a parish. In some cases such a staff contains presbyters, women and men religious, married deacons, professional directors of Christian formation, music director, liturgy personnel or directors, outreach coordinators, and the like.

Introduction

- "Parish baptism sponsor" or "parish sponsor" are the terms we use for the trained volunteer lay persons who become the visible contact persons for parents seeking to baptize their children into a faith community.

- In the pages that follow the term "parents" or "couple" is often used. And yet there are many single parents today. Pastoral wisdom requires that all parish ministers be sensitive to the marital status of the person or persons presenting a child for baptism.

Many of the social scientists of the 1990s tell us that most people will not change their attitudes or behavior unless they can either feel they must abandon past practices at all cost, or unless they can foresee some of the benefits inherent in such a change. The same is true regarding preparation for, celebration of, and reflection on the sacrament of baptism with infants. Parishes and communities content with their own practice should live in peace! However, those who are seriously troubled by the present conditions under which the sacraments of initiation are presented and those having a deep desire to better these conditions are, in fact, ready for a change.

The approach we propose has several stages which we will now explain.

Introduction

Shaping a Vision

We begin by forming a small group of people who will shape and formulate the elements of a renewed infant baptism process.

But before doing so, it will be good to know approximately how many infants are baptized each year in a particular faith community. You might do a five-year average for your own parish and, if you are located near other worshiping communities, you might like to compare figures. This will give some indication of the number of infants and families whom you can expect to meet, welcome, nurture, and with whom you will reflect. This information will also indicate the number of baptismal parish sponsors who will eventually be required.

The purpose of a steering committee or "think tank" is to shape and formulate the elements of a renewed infant baptism process. At this juncture six or eight enthusiastic persons, such as pastoral staff members and some hand-picked interested parishioners or community members, will help ground this project in reality. A small group as opposed to a large group, often makes people more comfortable about making suggestions or offering opinions.

The meeting should begin with song, a reading from the Bible (either a pericope concerning baptism or a lectionary selection from the coming Sunday) and a discussion question drawn from the Scripture.

For example, on one occasion, we began with the song "Seek the Lord," followed by a proclamation of Matthew 28:16-20 (lectionary 59). This gospel concerns Jesus' command to go forth and teach, baptizing in the

"From the earliest times, the Church . . . has baptized children as well as adults. Our Lord said: 'Unless a man is reborn in water and the Holy Spirit, he cannot enter the kingdom of God.' The Church has always understood that these words mean that children should not be deprived of baptism, because they are baptized in the faith of the Church" (*Rite of Baptism for Children* 2).

name of the Trinity, and assures us of Jesus' constant presence in our lives. The lector/reader proclaims the selection twice, allowing twenty seconds between proclamations for the group to "digest" the word, and providing a second opportunity to hear what was missed the first time.

Using this reading as a basis, one of the members created a discussion or faith-sharing question:

> I'd like to invite you tonight to name some of the most important things your parents or grandparents taught you, and which ones you would most want to hand on to a child today. Let's take thirty seconds to formulate a response quietly and individually . . . now, let's turn to one another in pairs and begin to share our thoughts.

Then, go to work! Use an orderly and complete process that allows the participants to express themselves.

Our experience shows that providing a short intelligible statement for each person to complete one or more times during a planning process enhances the spirit of launching such an enterprise; it also helps people focus on their common task.

FORM AN EVALUATION STATEMENT

First in this planning process is an evaluation statement:

1. Our Infant Baptism Program Has Been . . .

The participants are encouraged to address their remarks to the facilitator, while the recorder writes down all comments legibly, permitting no editorial comments from anyone. That is, no person's thought is corrected, ridiculed, or scrutinized, although a clarification question from the recorder may be necessary sometimes. Otherwise, each person's contributions are simply accepted. Also, there are no private discussions occurring during this work time: attentive listening is the skill and gift here, in order to respect and value the comments of everyone. When completed, a vision statement is to be formulated. It reads as follows:

2. Our Infant Baptism Program Should Be . . .

This section allows all participants to *dream*, to imagine what it would be like if all the human systems

Shaping a Vision

cooperated with one another. For example, what *would* such a program be like if it could be "designed from scratch"? Again, all comments are written down, with the facilitator repeating the statement as often as necessary. The facilitator, who is also a member of the group, can feel free to contribute as long as she or he takes no undue advantage of the facilitator role. Then, all proceed to the next section:

3. Our Infant Baptism Program Needs . . .

Certain basic components, including but not limited to personnel and equipment, are required by any well-organized and well-run program. Parishes or communities having previously-existing programs in place can also reflect on the assets and liabilities of what they have done recently. These comments are likewise recorded and remain visible for the duration of this planning session.

IDENTIFY PRIORITIES

At the end of *each* of all three steps noted above, it will also be helpful to:

- observe the patterns or common themes in all the recorded data;
- prioritize what the group believes to be the three most important items;
- write down these three items on a separate summary sheet;
- keep this summary sheet visible so that the group's members have a global vision of their progress as they continue to work.

From this process of presenting open-ended statements and encouraging reflective input, participants will be able to identify the overall top priorities for the renovation, resurrection, or creation of an infant baptism program.

Shaping a Vision

Going Public

Preaching or at least speaking at Masses is an important means of garnering community ownership of and support for this venture.

Obviously, the choice of precisely *when* to preach or talk on the baptismal program must be an informed decision. The lectionary, containing the Scriptures and thus guiding our preaching throughout the year, will determine the most opportune time. Consequently, a presentation is best made when the Scriptures lead the preacher/speaker to reflect on the baptismal richness we enjoy because of Christ's death and resurrection. When such a presentation is simply a talk on a topic, or a sermon having no connection to the Scriptures or to the assembly who will hear the Scriptures, the impact and power of such a presentation are severely diminished.

We chose a Sunday whose gospel portrayed the healing of a blind person (not the man born blind during the "A" cycle of Lent—this Sunday has its own unique character). What follows is the outline from which we worked and improvised at all our weekend eucharists (Mark 10:46-52—it occurs on the Thirtieth Sunday in Ordinary Time, Cycle B).

Introduction:	the song "Amazing Grace".
Part 1:	experiences of blindness; experiences of a need for courage.
Part 2:	our current baptism program and why it doesn't work.
Part 3:	our plan: to welcome, connect and journey with parents of infants.

"The people of God, that is the Church, made present in the local community, has an important part to play in the baptism of both children and adults" (*Rite of Baptism for Children* 4).

See Appendix 1 for a more complete outline.

Going Public

Sample Bulletin Announcements Preparing the Assembly for a Sign-Up Weekend

WE NEED YOU FOR OUR NEW BAPTISM PROGRAM

All those interested in working in our new four-part parish baptism program can sign up in the lobby after Mass next weekend. The basic job description for working in this new ministry is simple: loving children and their families, and spending some time sharing your love for Jesus and the church.

You will visit and accompany the parents of newborn children as these parents prepare for, celebrate, and reflect on the baptism of their child. We will provide you with personal training; we will answer the top twenty questions parents ask before baptism; and we will grow together in faith while enjoying ourselves in the process. Come and BE church for others. Sign up!

* * *

OUR NEW BAPTISM PROGRAM NEEDS YOUR HELP

As you know from hearing about it during Mass, our parish is beginning a new ministry to the families of those presenting their children for baptism. In order to carry out this ministry, we need YOU! Yes, if you love children, love Jesus, and love the church, we want to speak with you. As Paul the Apostle reminds us, "you are ambassadors for Christ." Our sign-up committee will be in the lobby next weekend with information on the program and training sessions, including a question-and-answer session on baptism. Come and sign up!

Part 4: a short job description, and announcement of training sessions.
Conclusion: an invitation to journey with Jesus as the blind man did.

The idea of reaching out to welcome others in such a practical and concrete way may be something of a revolutionary concept in many places. As a result, not everyone will "get the message" on first hearing. It is also realistic to assume that not everyone will be present on the specific weekend when the baptismal program is explained. With people being as busy as they are today, even if they are present they will need ongoing reminders about this new venture. Thus it is important in the coming weeks to follow up on the initial preaching by building some momentum for the program.

One effective method is to recall in subsequent preaching what was previously mentioned. Consider doing such reminders at the announcement time (before the dismissal rite). Bulletin announcements are also helpful.

During the weekend on which the program is explained, have a sign-up table in the lobby with an informed person or two to answer questions. Get people's names and phone numbers immediately, while their enthusiasm or curiosity is still strong. Have a small information packet ready to distribute (including the material found in Appendix 2).

Speak at meetings of various church groups and societies about the dream of an infant baptism program.

GIVE YOURSELF PLENTY OF TIME

Allowing enough lead time to contact all these persons and groups is vital and is not a waste of time; it is an investment in the well-being of the program. No one can ever predict how many people will agree to commit themselves for a year to be involved in one or more of the ministries required for celebrating infant baptisms in a community. Furthermore, if having a team of persons working on such a project is a new concept for some of the faithful, extra time for catechesis may be necessary prior to bringing individuals and groups together.

Going Public

Obviously, it is important to keep mentioning the new program. Even after extensive preparation and weeks of explanation, some people approach with perplexed expressions and questions. They are like those who walk into the middle of a conversation and cannot figure out how such a conversation began, how they got involved in it, or where its final destination might take them. Repeat and repeat.

Going Public

Extending Personal Invitations

It is fair to ask whether speaking to the assembly at parish eucharistic celebrations is going to yield the number of parish baptism sponsors needed to launch a successful and grass-roots supported program.

In most cases the answer will probably be negative, and not for failure on anyone's part. The reason is simple: people like to be *personally* invited to a new enterprise or project. Many respond very favorably to the songs or biblical passages that speak of God calling us *by name* to be a chosen and consecrated people. Think about it: if the choice is between being a member of a herd whose participants are identified by their social security numbers and a community member who is personally valued for his or her divinely-endowed gifts and talents, which would you choose? Most probably the latter.

Every community has members who, on their own, would not imagine themselves being part of a parish's baptismal ministry; but should someone *ask* them to consider such an endeavor, their enthusiasm and imagination may well triumph. In working with people seeking to join the Catholic community, I once asked a woman who was "thirty-something" why she waited so long between her first introduction to Catholicism as a teenager and the eventual expressing of her desire for full membership in the church. Her response brought a chill to everyone present: "People from every religious denomination asked me to accompany them to services but, until recently, no Catholic asked me." So ask, and do it personally: we never know what treasures lie hidden till we open some doors and begin.

General Canvas Letter to Elicit Interest

Dear _____ :

We are writing to invite you personally to join a team of persons who will work in a new baptism program here at our parish. An information night on this program will take place on (day, date, time, and location).

Since Vatican II the people of God have come to recognize the importance of baptism. Not only is baptism the first sacrament we receive, but it marks a new beginning in the faith life of a family. Most parishes find that couples with infants do present their children for baptism, but that these parents do not STAY CONNECTED with the parish. Rather, they feel isolated or disconnected, and in some cases they simply feel friendless.

The hospitality of Jesus is to be imitated by every parish community. Thus we should welcome with open arms the young (and not so young!) families who bring their children for baptism. Why? Because this is what Jesus did: when his disciples asked where he lived, Jesus told them to "come and see." And it is for this reason that we need YOU! If you are gentle, enthusiastic about family life, and willing to spend a few hours helping couples and their infants feel comfortable in a community setting, we are looking for YOU!

Extending Personal Invitations

This call to you is designed to help us reach out beyond our already-established community, so that others may see the goodness and love God has shared in our lives. Walking as a companion to others in the name of Jesus will enrich your life and will be a blessing for our parish. If you are not able to attend our first information meeting on (day, date, time, and location) and are still interested in the program, please let me know by phone or in person. Also, if there are other persons you would like to suggest for our baptism team, do not hesitate to let us know.

Sincerely,

* * *

See Appendix 3.

Bulletin announcements (see page 14) looking for help may prove useful. But more importantly gather names from the baptismal steering committee, members of the parish staff, interested parishioners, and the like. Better yet, make phone calls and, when possible, follow up with a letter.

The purpose here is to invite people to an informational meeting which explains the program and the role of the baptismal sponsors (the nature of this meeting is explained later on in this book).

Be sure to publicize the exact location and starting time of this meeting so that those who want to attend will in fact arrive there. For unfamiliar surroundings or hard-to-find places, posted signs will greatly assist the participants.

And once a person has agreed to attend the initial formation meeting, be sure to follow up with a letter, perhaps giving more information on the specific content of this session. Also, ask whether these people might be able to suggest the names of others who might be interested.

Extending Personal Invitations

The Informational Meeting

Some might compare this meeting to the unveiling of a statue, or to the introduction and showcasing of a new line of automobiles. An enjoyable and relaxed atmosphere should characterize this gathering and, for obvious reasons, hospitality at this time is of primary concern.

"Before and after the celebration of the sacrament, the child has a right to the love and help of the community" (*Rite of Baptism for Children* 4)

PRACTICE NEW SKILLS EARLY

For better or worse, most people learn new skills by modelling the ones they see around them. For example:

- the leaders perform a new skill while the members watch them do it;
- the leaders engage the members in performing a new skill—and all do it together;
- the members perform the new skill while the leaders watch them do it;
- and finally, the members alone perform the newly learned skill.

Leaders who constantly practice the art of introducing parishioners and community members to each other will begin to see the fruits of their labors in due course. This positive networking can be practiced at any meeting, but it is of particular importance here. Those who will be asked to welcome, gather, celebrate, and reflect with those who might have little connection to (and sometimes little interest in) the "workings" of the church community can begin to practice such skills with one another immediately upon entry for this meeting. In fact, facilitating these introductions can begin in the lobby (or gathering space, narthex, and so on) of the place where this first meeting will be held.

BEGINNING THE MEETING

Begin the meeting by welcoming and then thanking those who are attending.

Then follow the principle of the three S's:
- Song;
- Scripture;
- Sharing Life Experience.

For example:

Song. An appropriate gathering song like "I Have Loved You" by Michael Joncas.

Scripture. The word of God: perhaps John 15:1-7; this selection concerns Jesus who is the true vine, what it means to have Jesus make his home within us, and what it means to be "at home" or comfortable with Jesus as our guide. Read the selection twice for the group, and pause for about thirty seconds between proclamations to allow a moment of reflection.

Sharing Life Experience. This is drawn from the Scripture selected, such as: "Recall and share an experience or a time in your life when you felt . . .

- connected to Jesus; OR
- disconnected from Jesus; OR
- at one with God in nature; OR
- powerless; OR
- in need of personal pruning or a real "shaping up!" OR
- the need to be rescued from yourself or another force.

If you are unfamiliar with this method, have courage! When given the opportunity, the majority of believers will begin to talk, particularly if the question is non-threatening and does not demand or coerce false intimacy or easy familiarity. And yes, individuals are free to skip this section if it causes them discomfort.

The Informational Meeting

However, the invitation to participate is still vital, because of the nature of the program that will be explained in the sessions to come.

Our parish often uses an icebreaker exercise. We ask the group to *think* about a question that is posed. For example:

> For our sharing today, think back to your earliest days in this parish (or faith community). Think about *how long* it took you to feel "at home" here. Try to identify *what* made you feel comfortable here. Let's take about thirty seconds to reflect on these things.

Then, after thirty seconds or so, restate the issue:

> I've asked you to think about *how long* it took before you became comfortable here in the parish (or faith community) and some of the things that made you feel comfortable. Would you please choose one another person, and share that event and process with him or her.

Be sure that everyone is included in this process, and that no one is left out.

Give the group five or so minutes to share in pairs. Then invite any and all to call out the qualities that made them feel comfortable; have someone record the comments, in alternate colors to enhance visibility. (If possible, share this information with the community-at-large; it is reassuring for its members to know that their religious ancestors *did* accomplish some positive spiritual building in years past.)

EXPLAIN WHAT'S TO COME

At this time, outline the plan for the remainder of this particular meeting:

- describe the present parish process for infant baptism; list its drawbacks;
- describe the new method and outline its steps;
- present a general job description of a parish baptismal sponsor;
- answer any questions;
- announce dates for sponsor formation sessions.

The Informational Meeting

GROUP DISCUSSION

The next step is to divide the participants into groups of four (quads). Then ask the group these questions:

- what was this parish/community *for you* when you arrived?
- what do you remember about the first people you met?

Listen to some of the responses. Then continue:

In some cases, the first persons we meet in a new location are warm, friendly, hospitable, and memorable. In other cases, maybe not! The Roman Catholic Church is only now recovering some of its early biblically-based notions of hospitality, things that many Christians of other church communions have known for years. In fact, a person who has had the experience of being welcomed and treated like royalty upon arrival needs no more convincing. But even for those who do not believe in the value of extending themselves for strangers (be sure you are not invited to their homes!), there is a pragmatic wisdom in doing so. In short, if we do not get people here to the place where our community celebrates, we cannot talk to them, can we?

And what have we done to welcome the stranger and alien, the dispossessed and disenfranchised, the disaffected and alienated? What do they encounter when they approach the church after a lengthy absence? How often are they left without a clue as to what to do or which direction to go? Examine this scenario (it is a composite from several parishes) of what happens to many parents seeking baptism for their infant children:

- often enough, they don't even know where the church is, much less the rectory;
- because life today is hectic, they don't always hear a voice that is friendly on the other end of the telephone when they call for information;
- if they go to the rectory, they feel isolated and alone; for most people rectories are unfamiliar and strange places;

The Informational Meeting

- on the night of the "preparation class" the parents arrive and leave without getting to know anyone else; there are no introductions and no sharing of experiences—just the facts of the matter are treated;
- only one or two individuals give the presentation, which is in lecture form—decidedly not the way adults learn best;
- quite often the parents' attitude is to do almost anything to get the child baptized;
- there is no follow-up after the baptism; few couples choose to stay connected, and the parish is ill-prepared to reach out to keep and value them.

Now, what is wrong with this picture? How can it be improved?

Let the participants speak. Then continue:

In addition to some of the obvious failures in this situation, it is important to reflect on how hard it is for some people to open up. The world is divided among persons who process their relationship with the world internally before speaking forth, and others who naturally speak aloud and who deal with questions and issues in the external form as their means of working toward solutions. Further, imagine how hard it must be for couples who are not connected to any community, much less their parish church or the church of their nuclear family, to begin to voice their thoughts. Also, in how many other circumstances are persons asked to share thoughts on or reveal what they truly believe on an issue?

By contrast:

- the Scriptures record Jesus' command to his disciples: "Go and baptize all nations"; we know that Jesus is with us till the end of time (Mt 28:19);
- in the documents of Vatican II the church teaches that it is our active duty to inspire all people to a true and living faith and covenant in Jesus Christ;
- the Rite of Christian Initiation of Adults says that it is the community's task to welcome persons to membership, or initiation into church;

The Informational Meeting

- according to *Environment and Art in Catholic Worship*, published by the Bishops of the United States, the welcoming assembly (the community or parish) is the most important symbol; the *entire* parish community is responsible for seeking out and nurturing new members with whom to share faith.

OUR NEW APPROACH

In light of this we can envision a different scenario, one followed by our new parish baptismal program; it has four parts or stages:

- **WELCOMING** the parents and infant in their home;
- **GATHERING** at the parish with other parents and infants;
- **CELEBRATING** baptism during a Sunday or Saturday evening eucharist;
- **REFLECTING** on the celebration in a follow-up session.

As needed, give further details in regard to the steps of the process. Perhaps this would be a good time to distribute the outline of the process given in Appendix 2.

One of the obvious differences between this program and others is the presence of the infant at all four sessions. Some parishes advise parents to come for baptismal preparation during pregnancy time. This model emphasizes sacramental preparation as one requirement among many that can be accomplished easily in advance. Our program, however, is different. We as a parish community believe that the infant *should* be present for *all* the experiences connected with his or her baptism because the infant is the reason why we are getting to know one another better.

Also, the richness of this new life and the relationships of parents and child to God and one another cannot be exhausted in a simple "one size fits all" lecture which fails to respect the individuality and uniqueness of various family systems. Further, there is a short prayer service and liturgical symbol

The Informational Meeting

connected to each of these four segments. Each session will assist the parents to focus more clearly and without interruption on the relationship they and their child enjoy as persons blessed by God.

The purpose of this meeting is not only to explain the program but to recruit parish baptismal sponsors. But what does a job description for a parish baptism sponsor look or sound like? Some of the action words that describe the services these people will be providing in the introductory session in people's homes include the following: *welcoming, greeting, visiting, encouraging, connecting, informing, discussing, faith-sharing, facilitating, supporting, interviewing, praying, blessing, clarifying, calming, listening.*

Jesus did all of these things in ordinary circumstances, and people not only were touched by his care but they *remembered* these actions. In their hearts, they recorded the experience of Jesus who spent quality time with them: his outreach made an enduring impression on them. As persons with gifts to share, baptismal sponsors are a blessing for others as well.

Baptismal sponsors are called to be real listeners. And real listeners refrain from talking *down to* or *at* people, from analyzing others, from sounding like the one who has or is ready to give all the answers, from asking probing or "busybody" questions. In short, listeners are those who respect the uniqueness of others, who care about the struggles and concerns others face while recognizing that it's *their* problem.

CONCLUDING THE MEETING

In conclusion, allow for questions and answers; give an opportunity for those who wish to be baptismal sponsors to indicate this; give reminders as to the dates of the formation sessions.

Be sure to thank everyone for coming to the meeting; tell them that you look forward to the formation sessions for those who have agreed to be baptismal sponsors.

A Thank You Letter to Those Who Have Agreed to be Baptismal Sponsors

Dear _____ :

I write to thank you for two things: first, for coming to our recent information night on forming parish baptism sponsors; and second, for saying "yes" to our invitation to come to three formation sessions.

We as a pastoral staff are encouraged and grateful for your prompt response to our appeal. We know that you have many responsibilities and demands upon your time. Thus we are heartened that you will make the time to participate as a leader in this new parish ministry.

Just a reminder: the training sessions will run from (beginning time) to (ending time) at (location) the following (days, nights):

1. (day, date)
2. (day, date)
3. (day, date)

Also, as we requested at our information night, if you are aware of other persons who might be interested in our new baptism program, we will contact them directly. Let us know who they are, either personally after weekend Masses or by filling in and tearing off the coupon below.

Again, we are grateful to God and to you for the privilege of being able to serve the Catholic Community here at (name of parish). In all our tasks and our responsibilities, in all our sorrows and joys, may the Lord bless the work of our hands.

Sincerely,

PROSPECTIVE PARISH
BAPTISM SPONSORS

Name _____
Name _____
Name _____

Your Name _____

The Informational Meeting

A Letter to Those Declining to Serve as Parish Baptism Sponsors

Dear _____ :

Although I am sorry that you will not be able to join our parish's baptismal sponsor group at this time, I am grateful for your response to our invitation.

Should you find that your time, schedule, and other commitments in the future permit you to participate in this ministry, please let our parish secretary (name) know. We will be glad to have you join us.

Also, if you are aware of others who might be interested in our new baptism program, we will contact them directly. As you know, we are looking for additional persons who love Jesus and who are willing and able to share that love. Let us know who they are, either personally after weekend Masses or by filling in and tearing off the coupon below.

Again, we are grateful to God and to you for the privilege of being able to serve the people of God here at (name of parish). In all our duties and responsibilities, in our sorrows and joys, may the Lord prosper the work of our hands.

Sincerely,

— — — — — — — — — —

PROSPECTIVE PARISH
BAPTISM SPONSORS

Name _____
Name _____
Name _____
     Your Name _____

Consider inviting the participants to join with you in a circle for a short closing prayer; follow up with refreshments.

After the meeting send a letter both to those who have agreed to be sponsors as well as those who have declined to do so.

The Informational Meeting

Sponsor Formation: Introduction

Each sponsor session begins with song, Scripture, and faith-sharing. This format can also be used at many types of parish meetings. Participants experience a focusing as well as a conversion.

This opening process (song, Scripture, faith-sharing) accomplishes what the gathering song at the eucharist attempts to do, namely, to forge and underscore the bonds of unity which we enjoy by God's Holy Spirit in our diversity.

The terms "sharing" or "faith-sharing" may have acquired negative connotations for some persons. In this context, we simply give people the opportunity to connect a scripture-based experience or teaching with their own experience. Helping people to name and connect their life experiences with those of others empowers us to celebrate the presence of God which links us together.

It is important that the pastoral staff provide more than one person to speak at each of the sessions. We use the word "facilitator" in the following description of these sessions; feel free and creative in dividing up leadership tasks among several persons, according to their expertise.

Using a simple ice-breaker may prove helpful at these sessions (especially the opening session). Ice-breakers facilitate the group's bonding process and also help to diminish any initial anxiety.

Try one of the following:

- You are going to a desert island and can take only ten items. Which items would you take and why? If a storm came and you could save only

---

"Parish priests . . ., with the assistance of catechists or other qualified laypersons, have the duty of preparing the parents and godparents of children through appropriate pastoral guidance . . ." (*Christian Initiation: General Introduction* 13.)

See Lyman Coleman's *Serendipity* or any similar resource.

three items, which three of the ten would you save and why?

- Identify from your wallet or purse: the most valuable item, the most useless item, the item with the most meaning for you.

- People have described various experiences as "heaven on earth" or "hell on earth." What would "heaven on earth" be like for you and why? What would "hell on earth" be like for you and why?

**Sponsor Formation:
Introduction**

Sponsor Formation: Session One

INTRODUCTION

Song: "Now Thank We All Our God"
Scripture: Luke 3:15-16, 21-22 or a parallel account (lectionary 21)
Suggestions for Sharing:

Tonight we heard God speak about Jesus with the words: "This is my son in whom I am well pleased." Why don't we take a minute to think about *one* particular child whom we have experienced and loved . . . And after we've chosen and focused on one child to think about, name and describe (facilitator chooses *one* of the following sharing questions)

- what really pleases you about that child? OR
- what do you ponder and wonder about that child? OR
- what do you see in that child that you *know* pleases God? OR
- what *awesome* quality do you see in that child?

Why don't we take thirty seconds to think individually and quietly about that child and (restate the question)? . . . Now, let's break into groups of

"Holy Church of God, stretch
 out your hand
and welcome your children
newborn of water
and of the Spirit of God"
(*Rite of Baptism for Children* 243).

three, and describe to one another that child whom we love?"

After this experience, the facilitator may request a minute or two of feedback from the entire group. This segment of the session may be closed with an antiphonal psalm of praise to the God who works wonders. The texts of Psalms 145-150 work well.

See Appendix 4.

LISTENING SKILLS

See Appendix 26.

Listening skills are critical in this program, and the three-page listening skills packet will provide one practical method and inspire other possible ways of dealing with the issue. In our own time—with the simultaneous rapid development of technological tools and of a feeling that we are becoming increasingly isolated from one another—some social theorists are beginning to question whether human communication will be possible in decades to come. We also believe that, whereas some people are more gifted as listeners, all of us can in fact grow to become more skilled listeners who better comprehend and respond to others in everyday life.

Listening places us at the service of others. That is, we lose a bit of our self-concern while concentrating on the needs of others. Listening helps us to bridge the gaps between persons, and to share the God-given charisms of graciousness and hospitality, even when we are in someone else's home and not hosting a gathering.

USING THE SKILLS SHEET

In looking at the skills sheets:

• On **PAGE 1** there are symbols representing the types of persons with whom I associate. The facilitator can have each individual participant identify at least one person in each of the five categories, asking whom in your life do you see as:

— an *ear*, as someone who *listens* to you, your progress or problems?
— a *heart*, as someone who *shares from the heart* with you?

Sponsor Formation: Session One

- a pair of *lips*, a bona-fide *talker* with something to say about everything?
- a *pointing hand*, someone who's ready to give you directions or advice?
- a *magnifying glass*, someone who *examines* or *analyzes* everything?

The facilitator might allow ten to fifteen minutes for this exercise, and then invite the group into dyads or triads to share whatever the participants feel comfortable sharing. Since this exercise is designed to surface the qualities of a good listener, the facilitator should encourage the participants to share the *ear* in their lives first whenever possible.

• **PAGE 2** of the packet is an input piece on reflective listening. The facilitator should do some role-playing to provide illustrations for each item on the page. For example: the facilitator might speak for a minute and then ask participants to use the *description* function by feeding back to him or her what they heard the facilitator say. Emphasize the importance, especially at the beginning of the feedback, of using statements like *You think that*... or *You feel that*... This will be good practice for later on. Likewise, have the facilitator illustrate *responding* skills by asking a volunteer to describe a pleasant event in her or his life. Let the group describe it from either the *thought* or *feeling* perspective, or do each in turn. Demonstrating *attending* and *following* skills will not only provide useful information and verbal patterns, but a bit of humor as well.

Here are several resource stories illustrating the processes of *listening to* and *hearing* another person.

> Remember that fairy tale about the woman (it could have been a man as well, of course!) who asked the mirror who was the fairest in all the land? And remember her contrasting reactions, both when the voice from the mirror told her she was most beautiful and when she learned she was not? Couched in that story is also the issue of reflecting back to someone else the beauty that the beholder sees. What bonds the lover and the beloved is an echoing of the beloved's true self.
>
> In another ancient tale there is a lover who sought the face and hand in marriage of his beloved, whom he serenaded night and day. When he knocked on her door and requested entrance, she always asked "Who's there?" As long as he an-

Sponsor Formation: Session One

swered, "It is I. Please admit me!" she declined his request. It was only after he changed his response one day to "It is your own heart that knocks" that the man entered his lady love's house. Understanding and identifying the needs and true good of the other is essential love and basic outreach.

• Using **PAGE 3** of the packet, the facilitator can help the participants by asking them to think about examples of recent situations in which they *now* recognize that listening skills either did or would have come in handy. Being able to name experiences that are uncomfortable, uneven, or those in which confrontation occurs, will enhance the importance of listening skills for those about to engage in this ministry of companionship and hospitality.

Before the end of this first session, the facilitator announces that the work between now and the next gathering is the *listening log*. This simple but effective device records the use of the listening skills presented and discussed, and can be included as ground-breaking material in the second training session. Also, the facilitator invites each individual in the group to privately identify one person to whom they will actively listen during the week. This will include recognizing and identifying messages contained in body language, surfacing some non-question responses that worked well in conversations with others, and recording some day-to-day practical situations outside the baptism program in which listening skills will be valuable.

CONCLUDING THE MEETING

The facilitator ends this first session with:

• a reminder to the group of the next meeting date and time;

• a shared prayer (perhaps the Lord's Prayer or a moment of silence followed by an invitation to mention things for which one is grateful to God, or a combination of these);

• refreshments.

Sponsor Formation: Session One

Sponsor Formation: Session Two

INTRODUCTION

Song: "Morning Has Broken"
Scripture: John 3: 1-6, about being born again (lectionary 761:6)
Suggested Reflection Question:

Nicodemus has an *ordinary* experience of Jesus in the gospel: no visions, no transfigurations, no voices from clouds in this story. But his experience of Jesus is a powerful one: by asking questions, Nicodemus shows he's interested in finding out more about this Jesus. Today's encounter on his faith journey leads Nicodemus to *want* to know Jesus more deeply and know more about him.

Perhaps you have met Jesus on your life journey as well; perhaps you've heard his voice in prayer, or discovered his peace, compassion, or challenging voice along the way. Consider the encounters you've had with Jesus in your life.

Why don't we take thirty seconds to think about a *specific* experience of Jesus we have had, and would share with several other people?

After the silent reflection the facilitator asks all to break into triads for about ten minutes to allow the participants to share their stories. Affirm from your own experience the wonders of God in announcing the Divine Presence through Jesus in so many different ways. The facilitator

"You call those who have been baptized to announce the Good News of Jesus Christ to people everywhere" (*Rite of Baptism for Children* 224).

See Appendix 4.

might even invite the sponsors-to-be to identify *where* they were (physical location) when they encountered Jesus. Again, a selection from one of the psalms might appropriately close this opening segment, since the texts speak of the universal majesty of our God.

REVIEW LISTENING SKILLS

Next, review the "homework" accomplished by the members since the last session. Dyads (groups of two persons) may be an effective way to allow participants to talk about their successful putting into practice of the listening skills from session one. You might like to encourage their sharing by inviting them to review the page marked "Reflective Listening" for just a moment. Then each person can take a turn sharing his or her experience of active listening, after which the individual's partner can reflect back what she or he has heard. If clarifications are necessary, so be it: active listening is both an art and a science, worthy of practice and development. It is a process, and the time it takes to develop an expertise is worth our efforts. Close this segment by again reminding the group that being ready to respond with *listening skills* rather than simply providing answers will pay huge dividends in the big picture of this baptismal enterprise.

THE PROCESS

No doubt some of the practical-minded participants in the group will begin to question or wonder aloud, "Isn't there any *content* to this program?" The answer, of course, is most certainly affirmative! However, we believe it is crucial for individuals to grasp the *process* as a primary piece. Still, it would be good to help them see the grand scheme of things: provide the overview or vision of this program, and then go back to do the pieces individually in detail. This might be a good opportunity to do just that. The outline of the process for parish sponsors (see Appendix 2) provides a simple overview.

Now go back and reflect upon each part of the process in detail, especially as it relates to the sponsors.

Sponsor Formation: Session Two

1. Welcoming

Those who study communication arts (specifically conversations) tell us that the opening remarks, introductions, or greetings and the closings, departure statements or sign-offs in which we verbally engage are art forms. Ask the participants what they might say after the parents whom they are going to visit answer the door. How might the sponsors introduce themselves? Perhaps they would like to practice on one another. Then, the essential issue becomes: "what do you say *after* you say hello?" Let the members of the group brainstorm their way into confidence, so that they know there are arsenals of appropriate responses in a home where an infant lives. You might like to supplement your own list with applicable possibilities from our list (see Appendix 9).

> Note well: we create a more comfortable environment when we invite someone to share by using open-ended statements rather than by asking dead-end questions that can often cause anxiety or by giving responses like "I don't know." Not so strangely, if this welcoming is done *well*, people will volunteer more information than you'll actually want to know. After all, how many people take the time to listen without interruption to us today? How many people give us their undivided attention? Parish sponsors can become welcome visitors to a household. Also, by using open-ended statements during the short intake-interview, the sponsor will gather the necessary information without seeming to be nosy.

The facilitator now invites the prospective baptism sponsors to imagine what the *welcoming* will be like.

- You will receive a call from one of our parish secretaries, who will give you the name and phone number of a couple or parent asking to having their child baptized.

- You as a parish sponsor will make an appointment to go to the home of the new infant.

For Sponsors: How We Envision the Welcoming

The following is a simple outline and reminder of the tasks a parish baptismal sponsor is to perform upon welcoming and visiting a couple in their home.

1. Greet and welcome the couple with the love and affection of Jesus himself. In this way they can see Jesus more clearly through you.

2. Listen to the couple. They may have wonderful stories of the ways in which God brought them together, has worked in their lives, and has given them the power to share that love in the life of their child.

Remember, listening is a key and perhaps the most important characteristic of a parish baptismal sponsor. Using listening skills is more important than having all the answers.

3. Answer any factual questions you can concerning the program and its purpose.

As implied above, you do not have to know the answer to every questions.

4. Record the necessary information on the baptismal record card.

5. If necessary, show the parents how to bless their baby, and encourage them to do so each day. Say the prayer found in the welcome packet (on the bottom of the letter to the parents) with the parents.

The text of the prayer is printed below for your convenience.

6. If you would like to add the Our Father and make the sign of the cross on yourselves as an ending to your time together, feel free.

7. Be sure to return the information you have gathered to the rectory or to the person facilitating the baptismal process.

8. Rejoice! It is the Lord who works in you to bring life.

Sponsor Formation: Session Two

Parents' Prayer for Blessing a Baby

Loving God, Source of Life, the gift of N. is precious and wonderful. Thank you for entrusting us with this gift.

Open our eyes to see our union in your creative power, and help us never to take this child for granted.

Thank you also for the power to bless N. As we make the sign of the cross on our child, we know that Jesus calls us to grow in his love.

Give us the patience to share Jesus' peace in our home, and help us to guide N. day by day. AMEN.

Sponsor Formation: Session Two

- Your baptism in Christ is your key and connection with the persons you are going to visit.
- You greet them hospitably as one person and one Christian to another. At the same time, you represent the parish and its pastoral staff on this visit.
- Remember the words of Jesus: "When you enter a house, first say 'peace to this house'. If there is a peaceable person there, your peace will rest on them; if not, it will return to you" (Mt 10:12f).
- You will engage in conversation with the parents as you encourage them to speak about their baby and his or her development and growth.
- At an appropriate time you will fill out a short intake card with them, recording such vital information as the names of the important parties (child, parents and their place of marriage, godparents, and so on). Your gentle caring and kindness toward them will help you to grow into ambassadors for Christ.
- As welcomers you will share with and explain to the parents the contents of our welcoming packet. For the content of this packet see Appendix 6.
- You may also ask if anyone in their household has any significant needs, such as food or clothing; whether there are any persons who are homebound and would like to receive communion or be anointed with the anointing of the sick; and so on.
- Assure the parents that you'll also be with them at the next three stages of the baptismal journey.
- You can then teach them to bless their baby if they are not already doing so. Suggest that they make the sign of the cross on their child in the morning, and when putting their child to sleep at night. Just as the missionaries of old have done for centuries in our Christian tradition, help parents to see that *they* too claim their child for Christ our Savior. You as leader will make the sign on the child's forehead first, and then have do the same. You might also lead them in the Our Father before you leave.

- Leave the welcoming packet with them, and be sure they know the exact location for the gathering session, and that it starts at (time) *sharp* on (day).

GATHERING

2. The Gathering: Joining with Other Parents and Infants

The gathering session is a meeting at the church for couples presenting their children for baptism and their parish sponsors.

The main roles of the sponsor here are:

- to meet, greet and assist parents and infants upon their arrival;
- to facilitate and lead the discussion segments of the meeting;
- to invite couples to share their experience;
- to support couples in their growing discovery of Christian identity;
- to help clarify any misunderstandings— regarding the church, baptism, or this particular program—the parents may have acquired along the way, either from other couples or well-meaning friends and relatives;
- to help lead them through the song, Scripture, and a sharing question;
- The rationale for this session: to observe the links we have to one another in our community, in households, and in our families of origin. By sitting and sharing with them, you will help them to experience a bonding with the wider community we call the church.

Toward the end of the gathering session, a priest or deacon will invite those present to join in prayer. He will then anoint the baby on the chest for the first time with the oil of catechumens—this is one

**For Sponsors:
How We Envision the Gathering**

The gathering is a meeting at the church for couples presenting their children for baptism.

As a sponsor, your main role at this meeting is:

• to meet, greet, and assist parents and infants upon their arrival;

• to facilitate and lead the discussion segments of the meeeting;

• to invite couples to share their experience;

• to support couples in their growing discovery of Christian identity;

• to help clarify any misunderstandings regarding the church, baptism, or this particular program they may have acquired along the way, either from other couples or from well-meaning friends and relatives;

• to help lead the parents through the song, Scripture, and a sharing question.

The rationale for this session is to observe the links we have to one another in our community, in households, and in our families of origin. By sharing with the couples, you will help them experience a bonding with the wider community we call church.

Toward the end of the session a priest or deacon will invite all present to join in prayer. He will anoint the baby on the chest for the first time with the oil of catechumens (beginners in the faith) with the sign of the cross (this is one of the preparation rites for baptism). Then an acclamation will be sung to close the prayer. Refreshments will then be served.

Sponsor Formation: Session Two

of the preparatory rites of baptism—with the sign of the cross. We will sing an "Alleluia!" or other acclamation at that time to close our prayer.

3. Celebrating: Baptism at Mass

You arrive at church at least fifteen to twenty minutes before time, so that you can help the parents and their families to their seats near the font. You are their support team.

- Mother and father sit on the aisle with one of them holding the baby; godparents next to them, and yourselves next to them. The rest of the family can be seated around them or, on days when many babies are being baptized, as close to the family as possible.

- You will probably function as the guide for the parents and families if they are not regular church-goers, providing them cues as to when to sit and stand.

- By the end of the homily, the parents remove the baby's hat.

- The baptism occurs right after the renewal of baptismal promises, and only the parents and godparents will come right up to the font for it. Then, they will return to their same seats and, while the parent on the aisle holds the child (unless neither parent is present), the priest or deacon anoints the baby's forehead with chrism.

- At the end of Mass you can help the parents and godparents with the infant by leading them as they join the presider and other ministers in the recessional procession.

- You will go out into the lobby where you may accompany the parents, baby, and godparents as they receive greetings and congratulations from the faithful.

[Can you see how community is built up at each stage of the baptismal process?]

**For Sponsors:
How We Envision the
Baptismal Celebration**

As a parish baptismal sponsor, you are requested to arrive at church at least fifteen to twenty minutes before the beginning of Mass so that you can help the parents and families to their assigned seating. Remember, you are their support team.

Now, some practical things:

• Mother and father sit on the aisle; one of them holds the baby; the godparents are next to them, and you are next to the godparents. The rest of the family can be seated near the parents or, on days when many babies are being baptized, as close to the family as possible.

• You may have to function as the guide for the parents and families if they are not regular church-goers; discretly indicate when they are to sit, stand, etc.

• By the end of the homily, have the parents remove the baby's hat.

• The baptism occurs right after the renewal of the baptismal promises. Only the parents and godparents approach the font. After the baptism they return to their seat; and while the parent on the aisle holds the child, the priest or deacon anoints the baby's forehead with chrism.

• At the end of Mass assist, as necessary, the parents and godparents in joining the recessional procession.

• Go with them to the lobby where they will receive greetings and congratulations from the other members of the assembly.

Sponsor Formation:
Session Two

REFLECTING

4. Reflecting Together: The Follow-Up to the Baptism

- This is a session to flesh out the meaning of what has taken place in their lives by the birth and baptism of their child. Since we have journeyed and prayed together and have a common experience to draw on, it is an opportunity to ponder and reflect on the movement of God in their daily experience.

- As in the other sessions, there will be a song, scripture reading, and a sharing question to start.

- We will "go back" through the ritual moments of the baptism ceremony from the beginning of the process—the welcoming, the gathering, and the baptism itself.

- As we take some time to linger over what we have said and done, the deeper significance of each stage will surface.

- This is also an opportunity to invite the parents of the newly-baptized to network with one another and to stay connected with each other and the parish community.

- We will deal with the issues of commitment and continuity gently and strongly, as an invitation which comes from you as representatives of the parish. Since we believe so strongly in the church as community, we invest time and energy here to make them aware of our need for their weekly presence at eucharist.

- Before concluding, we will light a baptismal candle for each child from the paschal candle (also known as the Easter or Christ candle). This is a graphic invitation to maintain continuity and community with us. We also pray for the mothers and fathers of the children and for all present, using one of the blessings found in the Rite for Infant Baptism.

**For Sponsors:
How We Envision the
Reflection Session**

The reflection session takes place after the baptism, and its purpose is to flesh out the meaning of what has taken place in the lives of the parents by the birth and baptism of their child. Since we have journeyed and prayed together and have a common experience to draw on, this session offers an opportunity to ponder and reflect on the movement of God in our daily experience.

As a sponsor, you will be asked to:

• help the couple "go back" through the ritual moments of the baptismal ceremony, including the welcoming, the gathering session, and the baptism itself;

• help the couple surface the deeper meaning of each stage of the process.

This session also offers the opportunity to invite the parents of the newly-baptized to network with one another and to stay connected with each other and with the parish community.

We will deal with the issues of commitment and continuity and do so both gently and strongly. Since we believe so strongly in the church as community, we invest time and energy here to make the parents aware of our need for their weekly presence at the eucharist.

Before the session concludes, we will light a baptismal candle for each church from the paschal candle (also known as the Easter or Christ candle). This is a striking invitation to maintain continuity and community with the parish. We also will pray for the mothers and fathers of the children and for all present.

Sponsor Formation: Session Two

ANSWERING QUESTIONS

After a stretch-and-refreshment break, this might be a good opportunity to list the questions the participants have about the process or content. The facilitator should tell the participants up front that all questions will be answered, and in a systematic way. Putting all the questions up in newsprint will validate the questions, not only for the person courageous enough to ask it but for all those who want to know but didn't have the confidence or the words to phrase the question. Keeping those questions visible will help everyone to remember the many concerns participants have, as well as their enthusiasm.

SOME DOCTRINAL ISSUES

Once the parish sponsor has spent some time getting acquainted with and showing genuine interest in the parents and their infant, filling out the baptismal information card is the next step (this is a relatively short and simple but important transaction).

As a background to the issues and questions that arise in many discussions on the subject of baptism, we strongly suggest that the facilitator present an input piece at this time. But before doing so, it might be good for the facilitator to ask the group to surface questions they think parents might raise during the home visits. Based on our experience, the six sections (a summary of our input) noted below contain issues that the sponsors will be facing in their home visits. We use the following outline and text for this presentation.

1. Introduction: God's World is One
2. Baptism: Being Connected to God for Life
3. Sacraments: Like Faucets or Muzak?
4. Limbo: One Among Many Explanations
5. Membership in the Church
6. Original Sin and the "Sin of the World"

1. Introduction: God's World Is One

Clarence Joseph Rivers, a black composer of church music and priest of the Cincinnati archdiocese, once spoke to a group of musicians about the music they

Sponsor Formation: Session Two

played and prayed with Christian assemblies. He reminded them that persons are whole and entire human beings, not minds, bodies, souls, and spirits without connections. Also, there is not one world just for Catholics and a separate world for everyone else, unlike the rhetoric of certain radio preachers and teachers of the recent past. In the same way, the formal distinction between sacred and secular music has not been too helpful. It would be like saying there is music for "this world" and music for "another world." If one actually hears music that is literally "out of this world," Father Rivers suggested, one should probably fall to one's knees and make a good act of contrition because God's angels were coming to claim you!

There's only one universe, and it belongs to God, and we share in it through God's grace. In that same spirit, the world is God's sacrament. In a poem by Gerard Manley Hopkins, his more-than-a century-old text ends with the words: "for Christ plays in ten thousand places, lovely in limbs and lovely in eyes not his, to the Father, in the features of men's faces." Again, just as Paul the Apostle reminds us that there are no longer Jew or Greek, slave or free, but all are one in Christ, so throughout God's one and holy world there are limitless persons and experiences which illustrate the wonders of God. As believers, we deliberately seek out and name God's goodness to us, and we recognize that being in a relationship with God is a blessing.

2. Baptism: Being Connected to God for Life

Baptism is a sacrament of initiation. Let's take this statement apart for a moment and put our ideas into a proper historical context. Recall the definition of a sacrament from the days in which our parents and their religious ancestors were raised: "a sacrament is an outward sign instituted by Christ to give grace." For its time, such a definition reflected our religious self-understanding and how we perceived ourselves. But as important as each element of the definition is (our sacramental rootings in Christ, baptism as an outward sign of an inward reality, our relationship and bonding with God), one key ingredient is missing: the ecclesial, the communitarian, the church! Membership in the church is a *personal* not a private experience, and membership always has communal dimensions.

Also, baptism is one of three sacraments of initiation (the other two being confirmation and the

"In the sacraments of Christian initiation we ... receive the Spirit of filial adoption and are part of the people of God in the celebration of the Lord's death and resurrection" (*Christian Initiation: General Introduction* 1)

Sponsor Formation: Session Two

eucharist). Initiation signals a person's entry both into the church of Christ *and* into the Catholic Christian way of life as celebrated in a faith community. Such an encounter with Christ, who is the sacrament of God, visually and effectively captures the process of conversion and transformation that is part of God's plan for each of us. Therefore, baptism is the church's response to Christ's invitation to live his life always. It is from the baptismal font of Christ's life that all our activities, liturgical and otherwise, flow. In fact, we move from the font to the banquet feast of the eucharist. We now see clearly that the process used to welcome adults, known as the Order of Christian Initiation of Adults, gradually leads new members through the church's initiation process. And in that process one becomes a member of the church when the church's minister proclaims this person to be a catechumen. In the rite of infant baptism we capture this moment in the first anointing when we make the sign of the cross with the oil of catechumens. Catechumens are beginners in faith, persons whose interior dispositions lead them to ask for admission to and membership in the church. Therefore, *before* we are baptized in water and the Holy Spirit, there is a place for us in Christ's body, the church. As we are signed and sealed, we see different persons serving each other in the work of Christ: child; parents; family; godparents; parish sponsors; diocesan bishop; sisters and brothers I've never met; even the pope! It's all about connections. Yes, connections.

Baptism is *one sacrament*, one way in which we celebrate the presence of Jesus Christ. The following true story may help us broaden somewhat our vision of sacraments. Dennis and Diane worked at a supermarket. Denis was in love with Diane but was afraid to speak to her. He thought that if he asked her out she might tell him to drop dead. So for an entire year he contented himself with catching peeks at her over the pineapples and through the aisles of Post Toasties. It was driving him crazy, so he finally got up the courage to ask her out. To his amazement Diane said yes! It turns out that she was in love with him for that previous year, and she was dying for an opportunity to get his attention, but was afraid he would have given her the brush-off! They wasted a whole year: imagine! Now let's ask Dennis and Diane the question about sacraments. "Since you were both in love with each other all the while anyway, what difference did it make whether or not you celebrated the

**Sponsor Formation:
Session Two**

naming of your mutual affection with each other?" What difference did it make? All the difference in the world!

This brings us to another mystery. Why did it take these two people a whole year to finally talk to each other? Why do we miss the presence of God in the world? Why do we see and love God, and then forget? Why are we like people standing on the back of a whale, while fishing for mackerel? Why do we miss the forest for the trees? The answer depends on how we see sacraments: are they like faucets or like muzak?

3. Sacraments: Like Faucets or Muzak?

Most of us grew up with a religious outlook that viewed the seven sacraments as the more or less exclusive channels or "faucets" through which God's grace enters the world. But we can rightly ask "what happens to those who are not put under the faucet when they're born?"

When they grow older, those persons could achieve a "baptism of desire," as it was called, because they lived good lives and truly did accept God's grace without realizing it. Or, for those who were sympathetic to the way of Christ but not officially part of the church by baptism, there was a "baptism of blood." By giving one's life for Christ, a person would receive the same bond of grace with God as those who had received it under the "sacramental faucet of baptism at birth."

This "faucet view" of God's grace entering the world, a view that sees the sacraments as being something like faucets of grace that one switches off or on at will, obviously has limitations. Although it is perhaps a useful image for young children, it obscures the more mysterious reality of God working in the world. We might consider another and better way of characterizing God's work in our midst, namely, it is like "muzak."

We have all heard muzak before, but we rarely pay attention to it. Imagine you are on an elevator. Someone starts humming the tune that is playing on the muzak in the background. Now you're paying attention to it and wondering what the name of the melody is. Somebody asks this question out loud, and now everybody is trying out titles until someone finally says, "It's that old Irving Berlin classic, 'If I had a nose full of nickels, I'd sneeze 'em all atch-you'." Then everyone says, "Of course, that's it! Now I remember that one . . ."

This is the quality of human experience we call "sacramentality." The music was always there, but when

"Baptism incorporates us into Christ and forms us into God's people. Ths first sacrament pardons all our sins, rescues us from the power of darkness, and brings us to the dignity of adopted children, a new creation through water and the Holy Spirit" (*Christian Initiation: General Introduction* 2).

Sponsor Formation: Session Two

we or someone else names it, we experience it differently. The *naming is the sacrament*. Take another look at the old definition of a sacrament: "an outward sign instituted by Christ to give grace." This is a "faucet" definition. We need to remember that, in all human situations, grace is already there, just like the muzak. God's grace is everywhere, wherever God is. Grace is God. Grace is God's love offered to us, everywhere, at all times and in all places. Unearned, freely given, the very self of God playing in the background and in the foreground and all around. Most of the time we don't even notice. That's why we celebrate sacraments, the "name that tune" called "the church." We say to the world and to ourselves, "God is playing everywhere, let's play and pray with God."

4. Limbo: One Among Many Explanations

Limbo was one attempt by some thinkers who viewed sacraments as "faucets" to explain what would happen if an infant who was innocent of personal sin died before receiving supernatural grace in the only place you can get it: the sacrament of baptism. During this time, many others still believed and understood that God would not condemn these innocent ones to hell. Instead, they theorized that God would send such infants to a safe place of natural happiness. However, in this place the little ones would not and could not behold the face of God. By contemporary standards it might appear that people thought the Creator was a less-than-fully-merciful God when it came to infants. Of course, not every single person in every age really believed that God would deprive innocent infants of eternal joy, but this "official" explanation remained as church teaching for a long time. The real problem was not God, or the infant, or even the failure to get him or her "to the church on time." The problem was a view of life that was too narrow.

At the other extreme, we find comments that many of us have heard from neighbors and family members: "But if grace is everywhere, why bother celebrating any sacraments? Can't we just stay home and do our own thing?" Many do, but after the next story perhaps the vision of which we speak will become more clear.

5. Membership in the Church

A friend asked her cousin, a young priest in a neighboring parish, if he would baptize her daughter

**Sponsor Formation:
Session Two**

Elizabeth, who was six weeks old at the time. The priest responded in the affirmative, delighted at the request, and proceeded to contact the pastor of his cousin's parish to obtain permission to celebrate the baptism.

After all the arrangements were made, the priest received an invitation in the mail from the infant's parents. It was a fine, gold-embossed envelope, the kind more often used for a formal wedding invitation. Naturally, the packet contained directions to a party after the baptism. When he had carefully looked it over, the priest noticed that at the bottom left-hand corner there was a printed message that read "private baptism."

The priest immediately got on the phone and asked his cousin what this message meant. "Oh," she said, "I added that because Elizabeth is the only baby scheduled to be baptized on that day." The priest continued: "But the word "private" confused me for a minute. We're not going to lock the church doors while we're in for Lizzie's baptism, are we?" "Of course not," his cousin replied. "Anyone is welcome to come for the baptism."

Then the priest asked the question that had been stirring in his mind from the moment he opened the envelope: "How many invitations did you send out?" "Oh, not too many," replied his cousin, "just about 125 or so!" Both cousins laughed at the curious irony caused by using the word "private" with so many guests invited. This was a public event *par excellence*, with clear ritual roles, responses, and responsibilities.

In the same vein, membership in the church is not simply a "hot-line relationship" between individuals and their God. As Paul reminds us, being Christ's body we are many members. In fact, Christ's plan is that all persons be saved and included in God's love. We see evidence of that wide-spread and all-encompassing love in our families, neighborhood, parish, small church communities, and in the world-wide church to which we as Catholic Christians belong.

Membership in any organization constitutes a definite relationship. If asked at what moment does a person become a member of the Christian community, most people would probably say "at baptism." Because of our work with the Rite of Christian Initiation of Adults, however, we have gained a more reflective and nuanced insight concerning membership. Since initiation is a process, meaning that it does not happen all at once, we are able to highlight and observe different moments of such a process. When a person's senses are

"Baptism, the door to life and to the kingdom of God, is the first sacrament of the New Law, which Christ offered to all, that they might have eternal life" (*Christian Initiation: General Introduction* 3).

Sponsor Formation: Session Two

signed with the cross of salvation or when he or she is anointed with the oil of catechumens as a newcomer to the faith, this clearly indicates that the person is acknowledged as belonging to the church in a basic way. As a matter of fact, adult catechumens—even prior to completing their full initiation into the church—are reckoned as members with specific rights and responsibilities. Therefore, an infant initially becomes a member of the church at the first anointing with the oil of catechumens. Whereas this may surprise some, it will assuredly be a relief to many, especially those who are concerned about issues dealing with God's mercy, limbo, and the like.

6. Original Sin and the "Sin of the World"

The term "original sin" raises some difficulty for many people. Whereas Adam and Eve saw creation in perfection, the rest of us have seen only a flawed or imperfect creation. Think of our environment and what we have inherited and live with. Think of the child who gets up first on a snowy winter morning: what does that child see? Pure white snow, undisturbed and unmarked by anyone or anything. Later on, people will begin to shovel and remove part of that winter wonderland; others will trudge through it on their way to work or school or the store. No one but the first child saw the world the way it was prior to tampering. In a similar way, to remove original sin is to reclaim our hope of seeing creation as it was meant to be.

Adam (which means "everyone" in Hebrew) and Eve were born without original sin! Imagine . . . This means that those who arrived first saw the world the way it was intended as created by God. They were created to be independent, in the image of their Creator who exists independently. The great difference in our independence is that our independence is "dependent" on God's freedom or independence. So God is absolutely independent and we are relatively independent. This comes across in the creation story by God giving Adam ("everyone") a limited set of choices. As the comedian George Carlin puts it, "You can't have *everything*: where would you put it all?"

Adam wanted it all. By making a choice that was not ours to make, Adam altered the original grace of God's creation. Adam tampered with it. What do you find when you open the back of your radio? A notification saying that there are "no user-serviceable parts inside," and that you are to "consult your authorized

Sponsor Formation: Session Two

electronic repair person or the manufacturer." In essence, by going back to our Creator, the Source, we recognize God as the only One who can restore us to that graced relationship we so desire.

In the rite of infant baptism, we recognize that babies do not commit evil themselves, but that they are subject to the Evil One and his influence in the world. Those who refuse to recognize the Evil One's personal presence need only read the newspaper, watch the evening news, or visit hospital wards in which babies are dying of AIDS contracted through one or both parents. The evil around us, the sin of the world, is a force to be reckoned with. So when we pray an exorcism prayer over an infant, we welcome that little one. We recognize the existence of evil in the world, while at the same time asserting the pre-eminent power of the Father, Son, and Holy Spirit.

> "Baptism is a sacramental bond of unity linking all who have been signed by it" (*Christian Initiation: General Introduction* 4).

> A summary of these points is given in Appendix 9.

PRACTICAL ISSUES

Parish baptism sponsors will discover a limitless variety of human situations when they begin to speak with the parents preparing for the baptism of their infants into the church. Some of the issues that will arise include:

- one or more divorces and remarriages, with or without a church annulment;
- the need to convalidate a marriage not presently recognized as valid by the church;
- selecting a name for baptism;
- previous negative experiences with church;
- negative experiences people have had with this new method of initiating infant members;
- requests for "private baptisms" and exceptions to established practice;
- special arrangements, like the participation of a clergyperson who is a relative or friend of the family;
- unwed mothers, unwed fathers, and delicate single parent circumstances;
- parents in the process of beginning, continuing, or concluding adoption proceedings;

Sponsor Formation: Session Two

- interfaith tensions: believers; non-believers; non-believing Catholics;
- godparents—their role and qualifications.

Naturally, some parish baptism sponsors, depending on their particular expertise and experience, will feel varying degrees of comfort in responding to these and other issues. We encourage our sponsors to know as much as they can regarding baptism and these questions. At the same time, we tell them that they are also free to respond in other ways when appropriate, for example:

- "I don't know the answer to that question."
- "I'm not sure about that."
- "I don't have the authority to make that decision."
- "Why don't I find out from the parish staff and get back to you."
- "We need to ask the program director about that."

Telling our parish baptism sponsors about these and other ways of responding will provide them with an inward sigh of relief and will do much to allieviate their anxiety. These volunteers are not expected to answer *every* question, any more than each pastoral staff member or church worker is expected to know every answer for the parish. There is great value in being truthful and "up front" about these topics and questions, particularly as they arise in the exchange of ideas and preferences. As time goes on, firm and reasonable policies that work for particular faith communities become obvious.

For additional issues and answers see Appendix 10.

THE WELCOME PACKET

During this session the parish's baptismal welcome packet is explained to the sponsors, each of whom receives a sample of this material. Whereas each parish will develop its own set of materials, a few words are in order regarding the welcome packet we have developed in our parish.

For the contents of this packet see Appendix 6.

See Appendix 11.

- Each envelope comes with a letter to the parish sponsor clipped to the outside. Obviously, this cover letter is not given to the family being visited, but is a simple outline to refresh the sponsor on the contents of this welcoming session.

Sponsor Formation: Session Two

- The sponsors have a slightly different variation of the welcome letter than the parent(s) will receive. Essentially, it provides an orientation to the process.

    See Appendix 12 for letter to the parents.

- The parish sponsors should fill out (*print*) in ink the baptismal registration card, and keep it in *their* possession until the gathering session. In our parish we have hand-added two items: the date the welcome session in the home takes place, and the date of the gathering session. We modify this card from time to time to include other data.

- The outline of the stages in the baptism program is a handy guide which will help the parents keep the overall picture and direction in focus.

    See Appendix 13.

- The donation envelope with an inserted explanation sheet is optional. Some parishes have taken a firm stand regarding this issue, eliminating the discussion of money and sacraments or church services in the same breath. Because people have continued to question us over the last two years about this matter and because many of those we encounter in our program are unchurched, our parish staff has decided to maintain it. In a note we make it clear that there is *no charge* for sacraments, and that any figure is merely a suggestion based on our experience here in the parish.

- The poem "If Children" is familiar to many people, and is helpful in reminding parents that their young one will not be an infant forever. Also, it underlines the crucial role that parents exercise in being present for and nurturing their child.

    See Appendix 14.

- The explanation of the sign of the cross by Romano Guardini appears in a book entitled *Sacred Signs*. It recalls in a simple but profound way how this Christian symbol functions on many levels.

    See Appendix 15.

    We have received permission from Michael Glazier Books to reprint this segment, and we are very grateful for his kindness to us.

- We have included a skills survey as one means of beginning to tap the giftedness of our parishioners. Putting such information into a file or database will be useful in the future, but it also sends a clear signal to the person filling out the form that our parish is an active parish in which we value all varieties of talents.

    See Appendix 16.

Sponsor Formation: Session Two

- Particularly for non-church-going parents, presenting a bulletin with names, faces, phone numbers, and some key information is more than a public relations effort. By including it, we suggest that newcomers might like to become involved in one or more parish activity, and that they are welcome to do so.

See Appendix 17.

- The article "If Men Got Pregnant" may provide some humor for persons and households who have experienced pregnancy personally or at close range.

CONCLUDING THE MEETING

End this second training session by:
- answering questions;
- providing a reminder of the date, time, and location of the next formation session;
- inviting the participants to share a moment of prayer together;
- directing participants to the refreshments.

Sponsor Formation: Session Two

Sponsor Formation: Session Three

INTRODUCTION

>Song: "Take, Lord, Receive"
>Scripture: Ezekiel 36:24-28 (lectionary 752:9)
>Suggested Opening for Sharing:

The facilitator might direct the group in these or similar words:

>Each of us has used God's gift of fresh clear water for different things in our lives. Why don't we take a minute now to remember a time when we became very aware of the importance of water as we were using it?

After a minute the facilitator continues:

>Now let's each share a "water story" with one another.

Participants now spend five to ten minutes sharing their experiences with one another. To help all gathered become collectively conscious of the many ways in which water appears in our lives, the facilitator can list on newsprint the places where the participants encountered water.

>OR

>Song: "Take, Lord, Receive"
>Scripture: Romans 6:3-9 (lectionary 790:4)
>Suggested Opening for Sharing:

>Paul reminds us that we have been called to taste death prior to the joys of the resurrection. Al-

"I will give you a new heart and put a new spirit within you . . ." (Ez 36:26).

though we are aware of this, it's sometimes helpful to focus on an illustration or two from our own life experience. For example, each of us has had to "let go" of certain things in our lives for the sake of having something better. (Married couples will sometimes say that they keenly felt the surrender of parts of their individual independence in becoming marriage partners.) Why don't we take half a minute to look within ourselves, and focus on one event in our lives in which we tasted death for the sake of life . . . Now let's share that event with another person in the group.

In this session, we need to look at two topics in greater detail:

1. some specific practical issues that arise from:

   - speaking about baptism with parents of infants;
   - being a baptismal sponsor, from both a personal and a ministerial perspective.

2. the nature of ritual, and the specific action of blessing a child.

PRACTICAL ISSUES

During the first session the facilitator listed on newsprint issues that the participants believed parents would raise while discussing baptism.

See Appendix 10. In our parish this series of topics has evolved into a more complete list which is now called a "Data Sheet on Baptism."

Our original list included such topics as:

- godparents and their qualifications;
- choosing a name for a baby;
- parents (an individual or couples) who are not married;
- single parent circumstances;
- marriages not recognized as valid by the Catholic Church;
- previous marriages and divorces, with or without annulments;

**Sponsor Formation:
Session Three**

- persons seeking to have their marriages "blessed" or convalidated;
- a couple or a person who has adopted a child;
- questions parish sponsors can answer;
- questions parish sponsors can refer on to pastoral staff members;
- encountering children older than infants whose parents seek baptism;
- different reasons why certain persons baptize their children;
- requests for "private" ceremonies;
- requests for a priest friend or relative to baptize the child;
- objections to our parish's method of preparation, celebration, and follow-up;
- resolution of conflicts between parish sponsors and parents;
- persons who complain about previous negative experiences with the church;
- interfaith tensions: believers, non-believers, non-believing Catholics.

The above list is by no means complete or inflexible: each parish, in light of its own pastoral circumstances and local history, will adapt or compose an appropriate list of "Twenty Questions" or "A Data Sheet" to assist baptismal team personnel.

Parish sponsors, because of their connectedness and rootings in a faith community, will generally feel comfortable about answering questions that deal with factual matters, for example: the time and location of a particular meeting, who holds the child during the rite of baptism at eucharist, etc. These and similar inquiries can be handled with little fuss.

However, it should be obvious from the outset that some people will feel less comfortable about—as one of our parishioners quipped—"representing the church with my definitive answer." Personalities are different; backgrounds and experiences are varied; and not everyone responds to similar situations in identical or even similar ways. Also, since each of us is gifted by God's Spirit in a different way, it is only logical that some will handle "off the cuff" questions more easily than others.

**Sponsor Formation:
Session Three**

Such situations can be further complicated, for example, when parents become outwardly hostile or defensive about participating in the program. Actually, it is not too mysterious that some people are more comfortable about expressing their true feelings about a church matter to faithful parishioners rather than directly to parish leadership.

The facilitator should be clear in helping baptism sponsors understand that they are primarily *companions on a journey* for the families of those to be baptized. Sponsors are not expected to know every answer to every question (who does?); nor are they the only ones responsible for the welfare of those whom God is guiding toward the baptismal font.

A parish baptism sponsor can, of course, refer specific questions to a member of the pastoral staff, and then relay the answer to the parents. In situations requiring the direct and/or immediate attention of the program director or one of the parish clergy, the parents and/or the parish baptism sponsors can directly contact the appropriate person to clarify matters.

IDEAS FOR SUPPORT

A prudent facilitator or program director will provide ongoing support assistance for the parish baptism sponsors. Here are several ideas:

- by the end of this third training session, have a name, address, and telephone sheet (perhaps containing other vital information as well) for each sponsor. This, in effect, is the beginning of a sponsor telephone chain.
- every three to six months hold a support session to allow feedback. These sessions will also encourage adult learning and provide yet another opportunity to demonstrate positive modelling techniques. By offering a forum for people to share their experiences, the facilitator empowers these sponsors to make connections with and for one another. It is also a good idea for the facilitator, program director, and parish staff to hear how the program is *actually* going, lest good efforts and intentions be rooted in illusions.

Sponsor Formation: Session Three

- consider designating a "lead person" (or "lead couple") who has pastoral and organizational credentials, to answer questions that come from other parish baptism sponsors. Like an 800-hotline, such a person can be an invaluable resource, especially when this person keeps a list of questions phoned in by others. These questions will form one of the agenda items for the first parish baptism sponsor feedback session, which might be held three to six months after launching the program.

RITUAL AND ITS PLACE IN OUR LIVES

Now we need to deal with the second piece, that of ritual and its place in our lives. The facilitator might begin:

> Take a moment and relax . . . Think of something that you do regularly or repeatedly, something that is "second nature" to you, something that you're not even conscious of doing, something you wouldn't think of skipping . . . Does everyone have one of those repeated actions? . . . Good. Now think of the famous questions every newspaper reporter asks: who, what, when, where, and why, and apply it to your event . . . Now share the event and those 5 W's with another person . . .

In a large-group setting, the facilitator might choose to keep a list of these experiences visible, so that participants might be reminded of them. Once these activities have been listed and this segment is concluding, it is important to state clearly that these actions are *rituals*, life rituals that we cannot do without.

There are various kinds of rituals:

- **personal** rituals, like dressing oneself in the morning, or the manner of preparing for sleep each night;
- **familial** rituals, like birthday parties or holiday gatherings such as Christmas or Easter—the ritual even extends to roles different people perform and where people sit;

Sponsor Formation: Session Three

- **communal** rituals—for example, at a baseball game we stand for the national anthem, we do "the wave" if we are so inclined, we cheer for our team, we take a 7th inning stretch.

- **religious** rituals which gather people, families, neighborhoods, and communities into one body. Baptism is one such ritual: it is repeatable, predictable; it has an internal logic and reason; it is about relationships, both internal and external; it tells a story about *us*; it may even have a bit of danger attached to it. Have you ever heard a baby scream at a baptism? It is sometimes at the edge of danger and *do-ability* that a person can even dance with God.

Listen to this quote from Anne Morrow Lindbergh's *Gift from the Sea*: "A good relationship has a pattern like a dance and is built on some of the same rules. Partners do not need to hold on tightly, because they move confidently in the same pattern, intricate but light and swift and free, like a country dance by Mozart. To touch heavily would be to confine the pattern and freeze the movement, to check the endlessly changing beauty of its unfolding. There is no place here for the possessive clutch, the clinging arm, the heavy hand; only the barest touch in passing. Now arm in arm, now face to face, now back to back—it does not matter which. Because they know they are partners moving to the same rhythm, creating a pattern together, and being invisibly nourished by it."

Obviously there are definite sub-rituals connected to baptism as well: how and why godparents are chosen; the importance of the christening party in relation to the baptismal celebration itself for the family, relatives, and other guests; whether or not the parents extend an invitation to the church, to the party, or to both; whether directions to the church are actually provided with the invitation; what kinds of gifts are given, and so on. For the moment, though, stay with the large picture and vision of ritual.

**Sponsor Formation:
Session Three**

Consider this story from Gertrud Mueller Nelson's fine work, *To Dance With God: Family Ritual and Community Celebration*: "Recently I saw some small children playing at the beach. I watched them stand with considerable awe before the grand ocean as it rose up in huge waves repeatedly and crashed on the beach. The powerful water was not to be rushed into lightly or with abandon. They regarded the whole drama in silence as they clung to their mother's legs. Then with a little daring, the oldest launched an age-old ritual which we can all remember having performed ourselves and which we can see repeated over and over again wherever there are small children at the beach. The child turned her back on what was too awesome, and she began to dig a hole. Her brothers joined her. They dug and scooped the sand until they had a sizable hollow, and slowly they allowed something of the great sea to enter and fill their hole. It became their mini-sea. It was a body of water that they could easily encompass and control. In time they stomped in the puddle and splashed with abandon in a way that they were not yet willing to do in the surf. Then the surf rose higher and swished into their hole, wiping out one of its walls. With a delicious mixture of thrill and horror, they repeatedly built their walls, and the ocean repeatedly washed them down. Their manageable sea always let in something of the unmanageable. This was a game that they were able to play at for a very long time. For them it was a religious experience. They had created a hole to catch something of the transcendent . . ." (New York: Paulist Press, 1986; used with permission).

Baptism is a ritual with epic and mythic proportions, like the old movie "The Ten Commandments" or the modern movie "Raiders of the Lost Ark." These are more than medieval morality tales, emphasizing the power of good over evil. The baptismal ritual is also at the heart of what the late Joseph Campbell described in his series on myth and ritual. In the baptismal ritual, we "act out" a

Sponsor Formation: Session Three

mythic story, which contains basic truths that are larger than life itself, with meanings that transcend the ordinary course of events. How is this possible? Because we both believe and say, during the initiating event, that the person being baptized "has become a new creation and is clothed with Christ Jesus." That is, an initiate does not return to the same spot from which he or she began the journey. Baptism is about a process, a movement from death to life, from darkness into the light, from isolation or alienation into community.

Because baptism is part of "the big picture" of our lives, because it helps us to explain and make some sense of the grand scheme of things, we believe it best to celebrate the baptism event with the entire community present. That is, we enact the baptismal ritual to tell our community and tradition's story at the time when we are most clearly church. God's people, the faithful assembly, is the most important symbol we as believing Christians possess. So, a public celebration of baptism during the eucharist, our chief prayer, is preferable to the baptisms celebrated at separate Sunday-afternoon ceremonies by persons who are strangers one to another.

Think of ritual gestures we do as Catholic Christians. What are they: at baptism? at confirmation? at eucharist? on Holy Saturday night? at marriage ceremonies? at funerals?

A RITUAL GESTURE

As a practical exercise to get in touch with giving and receiving a ritual gesture, and as a way of preparing to lead parents in the actual action of blessing their child, the facilitator might look to The Rite of Christian Initiation of Adults (RCIA). This volume contains a rite called "The Welcoming into the Order of Catechumens" which involves making the sign of the cross on the person (specifically on each of their senses) being welcomed.

Prior to this exercise, the facilitator should refrain from explaining what is about to happen, or its meaning,

Sponsor Formation: Session Three

or how it is going to be accomplished. By using an inductive method of adult learning, we *do* the experience first and *then* together reflect on the issues we discover.

Simply ask the participants to choose a partner and face that partner. Then, tell them that this exercise is an unrushed opportunity to pray with one another, and request that they NOT rush ahead of the group. From the ritual, the facilitator should pause after the first line of each sense to be signed. For example, "Receive the sign of the cross on your ____." Pause to allow each partner to exchange this gesture with one another. There should also be a pause *between* the end of each gesture and the start of the next.

At the end of the rite, ask the members how they felt, what they thought, which piece of the gesture was easier (giving or receiving it). This may help them appreciate what parents of newborns will be experiencing when the sponsors visit them at home. Then, look at the prayer for parents to pray over their child. The facilitator might demonstrate.

See page 36 above.

CONCLUDING THE MEETING

Conclude the third formation session by:

- answering any questions;
- going over, as necessary, the information in the welcome packet, which the parish sponsors will leave with each household they visit;
- going over, if necessary, the materials in the parish sponsor training packet;
- reassuring the sponsors of your gratitude, encouragement, and support in this pioneer venture;
- having refreshments ready for all who participated in the meeting.

See Appendix 6 for the content of this packet.

See Appendix 5 for the content of this packet.

Sponsor Formation: Session Three

The Welcoming Session

The welcoming session, the first step in the baptismal process, occurs at the home of the parents and baby. This is the only session led by the parish sponsor. The purpose of this session is:

- to greet, listen to, and talk with the parents;
- to obtain factual information;
- to answer, to the extent possible, any questions;
- to leave a packet of materials for the parents to read.

The structure of this session is fluid—differing according to the circumstances and the needs of the parents.

The following points are important:

- Greeting and listening to the parents are primary elements (this is the first session where the parents have face-to-face contact with a person officially representing the parish). The "human" element is especially important here.
- Answering question honestly and to the best of the sponsor's ability (the sponsor should not be afraid to say "I don't know" or "I'll ask someone about that and then get back to you").
- Filling out the baptismal information card (the sponsor should obtain all necessary information and relay any particular information as determined by the parish staff back to the rectory).

"Before the celebration of the sacrament, it is of great importance that parents, moved by their own faith or with the help of friends or other members of the community, should prepare to take part in the rite with understanding... The parish priest should make it his duty to visit them, or see that they are visited..." (*Rite of Baptism for Children* 5:1)

Welcoming Session

See Appendix 11.

- The symbol performed at this welcoming session is the signing of the child with the sign of the cross. A prayer is found in the parents' packet for this purpose. The sponsor prays it with the parents and encourages the parents to use it frequently.

Welcoming Session

The Gathering Session

The gathering session takes place in a parish facility. Avoid classroom seating.

A host couple, parish sponsors, and a facilitator all have roles in this session.

Host Couple. The tasks of the host couple are to:

- oversee set-up and general hospitality;
- greet people as they arrive;
- if necessary, connect parents of infants with their parish sponsors;
- direct people to seats, in circles of ten;
- ascertain that lighting, seating, and temperature are all appropriate;
- check with the facilitator to see whether a worship aid will be used at this session; if so, be sure that the book or sheet is available;
- see that the paschal candle is lit for the closing liturgical segment.

Baptismal Sponsors. The baptismal sponsors are to:

- arrive fifteen to twenty minutes early;
- make name tags;
- look for and greet the parents as they arrive;
- try to remember the names of the parents, the names of their newborn child and other children, and whatever will put the parents at ease;
- introduce the couples they are sponsoring to others who are present, especially other parishioners and sponsors;
- provide name tags for others who come with the parents;

As for the time of baptism, the first consideration is the welfare of the child . . . the health of the mother . . . Then, as long as they do not interfere with the greater good of the child, there are pastoral considerations such as allowing sufficient time to prepare the parents . . ." (*Rite of Baptism for Children* 8).

Gathering Session

- guide parents into the meeting room, help them get settled, and sit next to them (normally the infant is present from the start);
- before the session starts, give registration cards to the sessions's facilitator.

The facilitator, while waiting for the gathering session to begin, might assemble groups of three couples and their parish sponsors to discuss several questions.

1. What does it mean to be a "good parent"? What will you do as parents that your parents did when they were raising you? What will you do differently?

2. What story from your family's history (involving a memorable person or event) do you want your child to know? Tell us about it.

3. If you could have anyone in the world hold your baby for five minutes, who would it be and why *that* particular person?

BEGINNING THE SESSION

The facilitator begins the session with song, Scripture, and sharing of an experience.

Song: "Glory and Praise to Our God" or "Now Thank We All Our God" or "I Have Loved You"

Scripture: Mark 10:13-16 "Let the children come to me." (lectionary 761:4)

For the sharing that follows the reading, the participants move back into the smaller circles with the same people they shared with before.

The facilitator continues:

Name a good quality you already see in your child or in one of your children. If Jesus chose your child or one of your children to show the rest of us the way to act in the Kingdom of God, describe the action or behavior Jesus would admire most in your child.

After about five to ten minutes, the facilitator asks the parents to share with the group-at-large. Then the facilitator continues:

Gathering Session

Name someone you know who has maintained a child-like attitude or quality into adult life. Describe this adult attitude or quality.

The facilitator re-gathers the entire group and receives feedback on this segment.

INPUT

The facilitator takes the participants' individual stories and makes connections with the stories of others persons, with the Scriptures, with the church's tradition. For example, if the facilitator were to ask the group—

Describe the first time you felt the baby in the womb move. What was it like?

Or, for those who are adopting or did not carry the child:

Describe the first time you saw your child. What was it like for you?

Then some of the issues that might be mentioned are:

- the commonality of our Christian journey;
- the uniqueness of the personal call we receive from God;
- what it means to welcome others and offer them love;
- helping parents see themselves as co-creators with a loving God;
- how parents have already begun to sacrifice for the child.

After discussion the facilitator leads the participants in a guided meditation.

MEDITATION

The facilitator continues:

Let me invite you to close your eyes as we begin to meditate on God's love and on the closeness that Jesus plans and wants for your baby.

Gathering Session

GATHERING

Imagine that it's the end of a long day, and you're beginning to feel it. You're weary, bone-tired, can you feel it? Now it's time to put your baby to bed. You pick up the child, gently and tenderly, and carry the baby to the crib. You've just nestled your child into the crib when you're suddenly aware of someone else in the room.

You look up and it's Jesus. You're a little surprised to see him, but you're not frightened. You feel at peace because Jesus looks just like you've always imagined him. You see caring and compassion and love in his eyes, and you feel a strength and confidence with him being there.

Jesus begins to speak but even before he says a word you know already what he is going to ask. He wants to ask your permission to hold your baby. You feel comfortable with Jesus, and you allow him to pick up your child. You can see the love that Jesus has in holding your baby close to his heart. As you continue to watch this scene, you also remember the Gospel in which Jesus took the time to welcome and hold and bless the children. With your own eyes you see Jesus blessing your child.

Then Jesus nestles your child back into the crib and takes a step aside. You look down at your baby and you see only peace and contentment in the child's face. At this moment you're only aware of loving, of wanting the best for, your baby for the rest of his or her life.

In the next instant you become aware that Jesus is no longer standing with you. He's no longer physically standing there with you, but there's no question that you continue to feel his presence. You're aware of having more strength and energy than you did earlier in the evening. You finish putting your baby to bed, and you are at peace.

I invite you now to open your eyes.

Gathering Session

RESPONSE

The facilitator can now ask the participants:

Does anyone have a thought or feeling or impression after meditating with us?

If specific questions are more helpful, the facilitator might try one or more of the following:

- How did you feel when you imagined Jesus in the room with you?
- How did you feel when you imagined Jesus holding your baby close to himself?
- How did you feel when Jesus was blessing your child?
- How did you feel about Jesus being in you and close to you always?
- Have you any other hopes or dreams about what you want for your baby?

After any sharing, this might be an appropriate time to treat some of the practical details concerning the baptism itself.

See Appendix 19.

RITUAL PRAYER

At the invitation of the facilitator, the parish sponsors invite those with whom they are seated to move toward an assigned place (the baptistry??) for the ritual prayer component of this session.

The clergy vest, and an assistant dims the lights.

Once at the new location, the sponsors ask the parents to open the top button on the baby's clothing (both front and back) so that the anointing with the oil of catechumens can proceed smoothly.

The presider begins by singing an acclamation, which will be used throughout the prayer. Some examples are:

- "Celtic Alleluia";
- "Blessed Be God" (Marty Haugen);

Gathering Session

- "Glory and Praise to Our God";
- "Glory and Praise to You, Lord Jesus Christ" (Lucien Deiss).

The presider then asks the parents (and godparents) to stand.

Presider:
You have asked to have your children [child] baptized. In doing so you are accepting the responsibility of training them [him or her] in the practice of the faith. It will be your duty to bring them [him or her] up to keep God's commandments as Christ taught us, by loving God and our neighbor. Do you clearly understand what you are undertaking?

Parents and Godparents:
We do.

All sing the Acclamation.

Presider:
The Christian community welcomes these children [this child] with great joy. In its name, I claim them [him or her] for Christ our Savior by the sign of the cross. I now trace the cross on their foreheads [his or her foreheads], and I invite all here present to do the same.

After the signing with the cross all sing the Acclamation.

Then, after inviting the assembly to pray for a moment in silence, the presider says the appropriate exorcism prayer with its corresponding anointing prayer.

FOR SEVERAL CHILDREN

For full text see the Rite of Baptism for Children 49B.

Almighty God, you sent your only Son . . .

Or

FOR ONE CHILD

See the Rite of Baptism for Children 86.

Almighty and ever-living God,
you sent your only Son into the world . . .

The oil of catechumens is applied to the breast of each child in silence. When the anointing is completed, all sing the acclamation.

Presider
To complete our time together, let us now pray as Jesus taught us. Our Father . . .

Gathering Session

Presider
I invite you to respond Amen to each of the
following prayers.

When possible the presider extends his hands.

> May the joy which God has planted within
> your hearts fill you and your children and your
> children's children. R. Amen.

> May the peace of God which surpasses all
> understanding give you the mind and heart of
> Jesus himself. R. Amen.

> May the love which is God's power in you be
> shared always with the child(ren) we welcome
> today. R. Amen.

> May almighty God bless you: the Father (+),
> and the Son, and the Holy Spirit. R. Amen.

> Until we meet again to celebrate the baptisms
> of these children, let us share the peace of
> Christ with one another.

An announcement is made regarding the location of the
refreshments.

Gathering Session

The Baptismal Celebration

Children are baptized during the liturgy of the word at Sunday Mass. The following remarks may be helpful to the parish staff.

Renunciation of Sin and Profession of Faith

From the ecclesial and liturgical perspectives, the profession of faith here belongs to the assembly, and not simply to those who are gathered specifically for the baptismal celebration.

Further, the presider can certainly exercise the option of asking the parents and godparents to stand during the renunciation/profession.

An acclamation immediately follows the profession of faith. Possible options are: "Blessed be God," the Celtic Alleluia or (in Lent) the antiphon "Glory and praise to our God," or other Lenten gospel acclamations like "Praise to you, Lord Jesus Christ, king of endless glory." This acclamation is also used later on in the rite.

All should be seated after the acclamation, since baptisms will begin immediately. Good, clear sight lines for the entire assembly are crucial. Only parents and godparents join the baptizing minister at the font with the infant; the rest of the family and guests remain at their places.

The Baptism

Our community has emphasized the importance of the parents' role in presenting their child for baptism. Consequently, we urge that one of the parents hold the child at the moment of baptism. There will be plenty of time for the godparents to hold the baby once the anointing and white garment prayers are concluded. This practice differs from the one to which many

"In the actual celebration [of baptism] the people of God (represented not only by the parents, godparents, and relatives, but also, as far as possible, by friends, neighbors, and some members of the local Church) should take an active part" (*Christian Initiation: General Introduction* 7)

Baptismal Celebration

unchurched persons are accustomed, but we believe that by raising and explaining this issue earlier (e.g., during the gathering session), we better serve the intent of the ritual.

Some presiders, in an attempt to use inclusive language, have arbitrarily changed the baptismal formula to "In the name of the Creator, Redeemer, and Sanctifier." This change is not permitted. Using an unapproved formula could provide problems in years to come.

The acclamation is sung after the words and pouring of water over each child.

The Post-Baptismal Anointing

If there is only one minister of the anointing and many children are to be anointed, the acclamation after the anointing may be repeated so that it punctuates the whole action.

Clothing with the White Garment

A community might provide baptismal garments for the newly baptized children. The garment should, of course, have a wide enough opening for the baby's head as well as sufficient material to cover the baby's shoulders (making it a real garment).

The acclamation is sung immediately after the presentation of the garment.

General Intercessions

Be sure to specifically include the newly baptized in the general intercessions.

Presentation of the Gifts

Invite family members to present the gifts.

Announcements

The persons giving the announcements can remind the assembly to offer their congratulations and blessings after Mass in the lobby or gathering space. This might include requesting that family members other than parents and godparents remain in their places till after the recessional.

Recessional

The parents, godparents, and the newly baptized recess with the other ministers. They are thus in position

Baptismal Celebration

to receive the greetings and congratulations of the other members of the assembly.

And More

A parish that provides refreshments after such a wonderful moment in its history continues and enhances the communal impact of the liturgical celebration.

Baptismal Celebration

The Reflection/Follow-Up Session

The host couple and parish sponsors fill roles similar to those at the gathering session before the baptism.

Have an easel and newsprint ready to record comments during the session.

"After baptism it is the responsibility of the parents, in their gratitude to God and in fidelity to the duty they have undertaken, to enable the child to know God, whose adopted child it has become..." (*Rite of Baptism for Children* 5:5).

INTRODUCTION

The facilitator begins the session with song, Scripture, and sharing.

Song: "Sing to the Mountains" or "Sing a New Song"

Scripture: Matthew 3:13-17; or Mark 1:7-11; or Luke 3:15-16, 21-22 (from the Sunday we call "The Baptism of the Lord" and which some Christian Churches call "Jordan Sunday" - lectionary 21)

"A WONDERFUL THING HAPPENED..."

For the sharing that follows the reading, the parents gather in groups with the baptismal sponsors. The grouping might be different of the pre-baptismal session. The parish sponsor takes notes for each group during this session.

The facilitator asks:

What were some of the moments you remember from the baptism?

The Reflection/ Follow-Up Session

REFLECTING

What were some things that happened at the baptism that you remember, even little things that struck you at the time, or things that you remembered later on?

Remember that it is very acceptable if more than one person remembers the same thing in the group. This is explicit testimony to the power of collective memory. Our parish has also had some wonderful experiences using this process a week or so after adults were baptized or received into full communion at the Easter Vigil.

The facilitator, after a suitable period, calls the participants back into a large grouping, and asks each sponsor to relate his/her group's memories. These comments are listed on the newsprint. If there is something particularly striking, the facilitator might ask for an individual to amplify his or her comments. This section of the session may be called: "A Wonderful Thing Happened on the Way to the Font."

Once all the contributions have been listed, the facilitator may look for patterns in the remarks on the newsprint. In our parish we identify general categories with various colors, and then with words. These groupings make it much easier for the facilitator to make connections among the various comments.

Some items found in the group's comments and our own explicit connections are:

- **GROUP COMMENTS:** Baptism is a communal experience, one which goes beyond "warm fuzzies" to real connections with real people: parish sponsors.

  Connections: Baptism is a unique experience we share in common: from welcome to gathering, to baptism, to reflection and follow-up.

  Symbol: Candle light

  Ritual Prayer: "The Christian community welcomes you with great joy." Our life takes meaning and shape by being part of a community, and we discover the best and deepest parts of ourselves in community. None of us is as smart, as holy, as inspired, or as happy, as when we're joined together.

- **GROUP COMMENTS:** There is awe and wonder at the time of birth. We're born into the world and reborn into eternal life. It's one birth in two parts.

The Reflection/ Follow-Up Session

Connections: Remember the feeling you had holding your baby for the first time? How do we describe it? Being bowled over? Overwhelmed? In touch with the universe? Transported? There is awe and wonder in our relationships.

Symbol: Water.

Ritual Prayer: "N., I baptize you in the name of . . ."

••• **GROUP COMMENTS:** There are words and actions concerning which you have reflected. You have taken on an adult responsibility in the presence of God and the community of followers of God.

Connections: Remember the promises you've made: to help your child maintain those admirable child-like qualities which you strive to preserve in your own life. This is a promise to bring them and yourselves to church. But there is more: never forget that children are a precious gift from God today and always.

Symbol: Oil. Your task is to help ease your child into life's mainstream, to be your child's helper and guide. In short, as you are led by Jesus, you also lead children to see and experience Jesus in daily life.

Ritual Prayer: "It will be your duty to bring your child up in the pratice of the faith, by loving God and by loving our neighbor as ourselves."

The facilitator may ask if there are any questions about this experience, or if the church community can be helpful in any way.

The facilitator invites the parish sponsors to lead the parents and infants toward the font.

RITUAL PRAYER

After the clergy are vested and all are ready, the facilitator begins with a sung acclamation, one used at the gathering or at the baptismal celebration itself.

Then the presider greets all present:

The Reflection/ Follow-Up Session

REFLECTING

> May the grace of our Lord Jesus Christ, the
> love of God and the unity of the Holy Spirit
> be with you always. R. And also with you.

The facilitator lights each baptismal candle and says

> Receive the light of Christ

and hands the candle to a parent of each child in turn.

The presider continues:

> Parents and godparents,
> this light is entrusted to you to be kept burning brightly.
> These children of yours have been enlightened by Christ.
> They are called by God to walk always as children of the light.
> May they keep the flame of faith alive in their hearts.
> When the Lord comes,
> may they go out to meet him with all the saints
> in the heavenly kingdom.

The acclamation is then sung.

The ephphetha prayer follows. With small numbers, it might be said individually. Where there are large numbers, the presider says the prayer once with a hand extended over the children.

> The Lord Jesus made the deaf hear and the mute speak.
> May he soon touch the ears of these children
> to receive his word,
> and may he soon touch the mouths of these children
> to proclaim his faith,
> so that they and we may give praise and glory
> to God the Father, both now and forever. R. Amen.

The acclamation is then sung.

All are requested to stand for the Lord's Prayer.
The blessing follows.

The parents, while holding their baby, are then blessed.

If the first prayer option is used, have the mother hold the baby during the first section of the blessing. The father holds the baby during the second section. (Be

The Reflection/Follow-Up Session

sensitive to situations in which there is only one parents—in this case the third blessing option may be advisable.) In any case, invite the parents (parent) to respond Amen after each part of the blessing.

Option 1:

May God, the source the life and love . . .

For the complete text see the Rite of Baptism for Children 70C.

Option 2:

God the Father, through his Son . . .

See the Rite of Baptism for Children 70A.

Option 3:

May God the almighty Father, . . .

See the Rite of Baptism for Children 70B.

The rite of peace follows.

Let us offer one another the peace of Christ.

After the peace, the baptismal certificates are distributed; then the acclamation is sung once more.

EVALUATION

It is important that the baptismal process be evaluated—both by those who have presented the infants and by the parish sponsors.

Give people enough time to complete the evaluation at their own pace. And don't forget to invite them for refreshments and hospitality.

See Appendices 22 and 23 for appropriate forms.

The Reflection/ Follow-Up Session

The Past and the Future

REACTIONS: NEGATIVE AND POSITIVE

Because the church is a human institution led by human beings and subject to human frailties, we need to admit that not everyone has been persuaded by our vision of baptism or its celebration, the church as a public community, and the ministerial implications inherent in our approach. In fact, there *have* been several minor disruptions, some vocal objections, and several protests regarding our parish baptism program. Some issues raised since we began:

- breaking the infant baptism ritual up into segments;
- neighboring parishes which regularly celebrate baptism outside eucharist;
- having multiple baptismal celebrations during a weekend;
- celebrating baptism only during eucharist;
- including visiting clergy (relatives and friends) in the celebrations;
- scheduling and time-investment of parish sponsors;
- having the infant present at all four sessions;
- having parish sponsors unknown to baptismal parents going to their home;
- parents threatening to leave the parish because of program changes.

We have put the listening skills we described during the training sessions to work daily since we began this baptism program. In most cases, after speaking one-on-one with parents and answering their specific questions or objections, we find that their discontent or anxiety has greatly diminished. They better understood our purpose and rationale for the program, and we had acted responsibly in offering pastoral care. In some cases, the parents opted to have the child baptized in another Catholic parish. We recognize that the parents can choose to do so. Knowing that in some ways we were pioneering a slightly different sacramental approach, one which had not enjoyed lots of advance publicity, we certainly did not take any of the objections or questions to our program lightly. We know that no one approach to God can claim to monopolize truth.

At the same time, we have received many positive comments, especially about the role the parish sponsors play in our baptism celebrations. In some cases, the sponsor and the family have formed strong bonds (including dinner and an invitation to the baptism party) even between the gathering session and the baptism itself. Further, we judged that none of the questions or objections raised by our parishioners should discourage us from our primary goals, to reach out and offer hospitality to the parents and families of infants.

SPONSORS: HOW MANY?

In addition, our pastoral staff has been concerned from the beginning that we would have sufficient trained parish sponsors to visit the homes of our soon-to-be-baptized infants. When we have been caught short at certain times, we asked parish sponsors to "double up" and sponsor two families. On one occasion, we asked our deacon to hold a welcoming session with several families, since many parish sponsors were on vacation. Although these methods were neither preferable or anticipated, they became "emergency adaptations," ones which alerted us to get busy and start recruiting more parish sponsors. Based on our experience, we recommend that a parish plan to have more parish sponsors than it actually needs at the moment. If a community has the wonderful experience of being deluged with volunteers, send them out two by two the way Jesus did in the first century.

The Past and the Future

SECRETARIES: THEY ARE IMPORTANT

May we also suggest that a parish plan to spend lots of time with the secretaries or persons who will be handling the calls from parents inquiring about baptism for their infants. These front-line people are major assets and key players, and they must be fully informed about the workings and organization of the program. Even before the formation sessions for the parish sponsors begin, it is wise to work with those who will be answering the telephone. Having them study the program notes and asking for their feedback or reactions, asking them telephone questions by doing some role-playing, and asking how they would handle certain personalities will indicate to parish leadership how prepared the secretaries or telephone contacts are at present.

Type up a common text for all incoming phone calls regarding the baptism program. This will enable all inquirers to receive the same information. Start with something like:

- one of our parishioners will call you soon to arrange for an interview and welcoming session at your home;
- there are two group meetings for parents AND infants to attend: these sessions are held on _____ and at _____
- baptisms take place on _____

EVALUATION: WITH THE SPONSORS

After three to six months, hold a session for the parish sponsors. Sponsors are on "the front lines" as well, and deserve any gesture of TLC that you can provide. Begin with the three S's (song, Scripture and faith-sharing) and be sure to end with refreshments. In between:

- listen to how they've been feeling in this new ministry;
- make sure you hear both the sorrows and frustrations as well as the joys;

The Past and the Future

See Appendices 22 and 23.

- evaluate the program (content) and how it has been running (process);
- make note of suggestions, including personnel and scheduling adjustments;
- promise to send all parish sponsors a summary of these proceedings.

Some of the suggestions from our first evaluation session included:

- having the parish sponsor bring a small gift, such as a plant, baby picture frame, baby book to record signficant baby moments, a cake, or the like;
- exploring a more active liturgical role for godparents;
- having the parish secretary do a preliminary interview, so that the parish sponsor would know the family's attitude or degree of openness in advance of the home visit;
- having the parish secretary call a parish sponsor as soon as a call is received from a parent, so that there is as much lead-time as possible prior to scheduling the home visit;
- collecting some baby stories and facts to share in the parish bulletin.

YET TO COME

In algebra when one variable changes there is a good chance that others will also change. Similarly, we believe that beneath the shift to a faith-community-based baptismal approach are unseen implications which will require investigation in the future. Examples:

- an annual monthly follow-up celebration to a child's baptism;
- a personal letter to a child on the anniversary of his or her baptism;
- how persons are formed for the other sacraments of initiation, for confirmation and eucharist;
- what kinds of ties and connections we might make with those other two sacraments, such as a

The Past and the Future

personal letter from the parish prior to the child's celebrating first eucharist and confirmation;

- exploring how the issue of infant baptism might be somehow included in our parish marriage preparation program, and the nature of the relationship between these two sacraments.

We have enjoyed developing this program. And we hope that the overview of our program as given in this book will encourage your parish to develop its own people-oriented infant baptism program.

The Past and the Future

Appendices

Appendix 1

SAMPLE HOMILY FOR PREACHING ABOUT A NEW BAPTISMAL PROGRAM

There is a song whose words are well-known:

> Amazing grace, how sweet the sound,
> that saved and set me free.
> I once was lost but now am found,
> was blind but now I see.
> I once was lost but now am found,
> was blind but now I see.

Most of us have suffered from temporary blindness:

• have you ever been looking for something, and then found it right under your nose?

• or, for older people, have you noticed that the print in a book looks big in the morning and seems smaller as night comes around?

On another level, have you noticed that there are different kinds of blindness: I can be blind to another's needs, to my own goodness, to other people's viewpoints, or to opportunities it took me awhile to see?

Take a moment: think of an experience in your life in which you came to see the fuller picture of a person or an event, and what awakened you. Take about thirty seconds to think about it.

> As an option have the members of the assembly share their reflections with another person at Mass today. Allow three minutes for this.

That "Amazing Grace" song has to do with being reborn in God's Spirit; it speaks of an inner courage and freedom and peace that Christians share. There is a segment of our parish population that could use our courage in exercising Christian hospitality, welcome, and loving care. The people I have in mind are the parents and families who present their children to us as church for baptism.

In our parish, as in most parishes:

• deacons and priests have been both conducting the one-on-one interview with the parents and presenting the instruction sessions;

• although there are numerous baptism each year there is no scheduled follow-up session after baptism;

• many families aren't connected with the parish before the baptism and don't stay connected after baptism. The reason is that they don't get to know parishioners, only those who are often disconnected!

Therefore, our present program is not working. It is not helping us build a community.

Our plan is to welcome people and connect them with parishioners. And here is the way we propose doing this:

- We will go to the homes of new parents for an initial contact; we call this their **welcoming.**

- We will continue to have a preparation here at the parish; we call this the **gathering** of the parents; it will focus on the impact of the new arrival and help parents to see their child as God's gift.

- We will **celebrate** baptisms at Mass, one weekend each month, so that parents might have a community of love and faith to support them and to pray for and with their children.

- There will be a **follow-up** session; this will help the parents to network, reflect on what baptism and its commitment mean in daily life, and which will invite them to stay connected.

Now for the best part of this plan: for each child to be baptized there will be one person (perhaps two) who will greet and walk with the child and the child's parents (or parent) at all four stages. And this is where you are needed.

We invite all members of our parish to have the courage of the blind man whom Jesus brought to sight. This courage involves seeing, admitting, and addressing this need of walking with and ministering to the parents of newborn infants. We're looking for couples and individuals who are:

- willing to share their love for Jesus and the church;
- willing to be a friend to folks who may find community a new experience;
- lovers of children, and happy to be around enthusiastic parents;
- gentle sharers, who don't have to be professional instructors.

Teachers will work with all who volunteer for this ministry by providing hands-on training and experience. This is an opportunity to stretch beyond what we as

Appendix 1

church have experienced in days past. We need to begin signing up persons right away. I will be in the lobby as well, to meet you and answer any questions you may have.

The gospel ends with Jesus reminding us that faith is what saves us. We invite you to consider doing what the blind man did once Jesus had healed him: to follow Jesus up the road. May we serve the Lord to the best of our abilities.

Appendix 1

Appendix 2

OUTLINE OF THE PROCESS FOR WELCOMING NEW INFANTS: FOR SPONSORS

Some parishes advise parents to come for baptismal preparation during pregnancy time. But we believe that a child should be present for *all four* experiences connected with his or her baptism, because the child is the reason we are getting to know one another better! There is also a short prayer service and liturgical symbol connected with each of these four stages. Each session will help you to focus on the relationship a child enjoys as a person blessed by God.

The Welcoming Experience

happens at the home of the parents and baby. It is an opportunity for you as a faithful member of our parish to greet and obtain some basic registration information from a parishioner. This is part of the preparation for a child's baptism. As our parish representative (whom we call a parish sponsor), you will also leave some materials for them to read. These materials will include our invitation to the parents to make the sign of the cross on their child at least once a day. As a parish sponsor you will be a mentor and guide for those parents.

The Gathering Experience

occurs at the church on (indicate day, time, location). A member of our parish staff will conduct a session which will help parents to reflect more deeply on how active God has been in blessing their family with a new life. We will have some input and discussion on the changes which have occurred since their child's arrival. We conclude with the opening prayers of the infant baptism ceremony, specifically, the first anointing with oil for the infants as beginners in faith.

The Celebrating Experience

occurs on (indicate days and times). Our children deserve the very best when it comes to God's love, and we express that primary care when we gather at the eucharist. In the presence of a faithful and praying community and immediately after the homily, we will renew and profess our faith and the child will be baptized by water and God's Holy Spirit. After receiving the second anointing with oil (sacred chrism), we will continue with the eucharist. The community will greet and congratulate the parents and families with love (specify location) after Mass.

The Reflecting Experience

REFLECTING

will occur on (indicate date and time), usually a week after the child has been publicly welcomed into the parish community by his or her baptism. This session concentrates on naming the experiences and understanding more deeply the symbols associated with baptism, including water, the cross, and the oil. Issues such as baptism's communal impact, memories of the baptismal event, and the commitment to Christ and Christ's church will be explored. The session will conclude with the lighting of a baptismal candle for each child and a blessing prayer for parents. To keep their enthusiasm for the sacrament of baptism alive, we will invite them to consider joining two groups. One is our parish sponsor group, to welcome persons at future baptisms. The other is a group that meets every two weeks with other persons to share their life experience and love for Jesus. We will explain both groups to the parents.

"This is my beloved child in whom I am well pleased" (Mt 3:17).

Appendix 2

Appendix 3

TARGET LETTER TO INTERESTED PERSONS

Dear _____ :

　　Thanks for indicating your interest in becoming a team member for our new baptism program. Our parish staff is very excited about this opportunity to touch others at such an important moment in their family life.

　　We are holding an INFORMATION NIGHT on this program on (day, date, time, location). At this session we plan to do the following:

- sing, listen to God's word, and share our faith in Jesus;
- explain our present practice, why it's not working, and share a rationale for our new program;
- describe the contents of our three training sessions for team members, and our commitment to maintain a support system with and for you;
- answer any questions you may have as a result of the presentation;
- enjoy one another's company and some refreshments.

　　The three formation sessions for parish baptismal sponsors will run from (start time to end time) on the following nights:

　　　(day, date)
　　　(day, date)
　　　(day, date)

　　Again we are grateful to God and to you for the privilege of being able to serve God's people with you here at our parish. We look forward to seeing you on (date, day, time).

Sincerely,

P.S. If you are aware of others who might be interested in our baptism program, we will be glad to contact them. Let us know who they are after any parish Mass or by giving us their names. You can use the form below. Drop the slip into the collection basket or hand it in at the parish office.

PROSPECTIVE PARISH BAPTISM SPONSORS

Name _____
Name _____
Name _____
      Your Name _____

Appendix 3

Appendix 4

PSALMS OF PRAISE TO CONCLUDE OPENING SEGMENTS OF FORMATION SESSIONS

Psalm 145 (adapted)

ALL:
Our Maker is gracious and merciful,
slow to anger and rich in kindness.
Our Creator is good to all people,
and compassionate to all creation.

SIDE A:
Let all your works give you thanks, O God,
and let your faithful ones bless you.
The eyes of all look hopefully to you,
and it is you who feed them in due time.

SIDE B:
Our Savior always shows justice in action,
and holiness springs forth in every divine deed.
We call upon the Compassionate One in our need,
and we receive the truth of our God's saving power.

ALL:
Glory to the Father, and to the Son,
and to the Holy Spirit,
as it was in the beginning, is now,
and will be forever. AMEN.

Psalm 146 (adapted)

ALL:
My soul gives praise to the LORD,
I will praise all my days
the One who nurtures me.
I will make music to my God while I live.

SIDE A:
Trust not in rulers of earth,
for they can neither help nor save us.
When their spirits depart they are buried,
and on that day their plans perish.

SIDE B:
Happy are those whose hope is in God,
whose daily help is the One True God.
It is our God who made heaven and earth,
the seas and all that swim in them.

ALL:
Glory to the Father, Creator of all people,
and to the Son, Savior of the world,
and to the Spirit who purifies our hearts,
as it was in the beginning, is now,
and will be forever. AMEN.

Psalm 148 (adapted)

ALL:
Praise the LORD from the heavens,
Praise our God in the heights.
Praise the Creator, all you angels,
Praise our Worker of Wonders, all you servants.

SIDE A:
Let the powerful of earth and all peoples,
let the judges and those of noble birth,
let young men come together and maidens as well
let old and young alike give God honor and glory.

SIDE B:
Praise the Name of the Majestic One, the Most High,
for God's Name alone is worthy of our praise.
Above heaven and earth is the primacy of the LORD,
who has raised us up from sadness and shame.
Alleluia!

ALL:
Glory to the Father, Creator of all people,
and to the Son, Savior of the world,
and to the Spirit who purifies our hearts,
as it was in the beginning, is now,
and will be forever. AMEN.

Psalm 149 (adapted)

ALL:
Sing to the LORD a new song,
let praise rise from the holy assembly.
Let us be glad in our Maker,
let us take delight in the Ruler of Heaven and Earth.

Appendix 4

SIDE A:
Praise God's name with a festive dance,
let us strike up a sound with timbrel and harp,
for our God loves us deeply
and raises up the lowly with victory.

SIDE B:
Let the faithful ones be radiant with glory,
let them joyfully sing to God at their leisure.
Let the high praises of God be in their throats,
and may all who hear this celebration be blessed.

ALL:
Glory to our Mighty God, living and true,
Glory to the Son, our brother and Savior,
Glory to the Spirit, our guide and light,
one holy God, come! Bless us all
now and for ever. AMEN.

Appendix 4

Appendix 5

CONTENTS OF PACKET FOR SPONSORS

1. How We Envision:
   - The Welcoming (page 35)
   - The Gathering (page 37)
   - The Celebration (page 38)
   - The Reflecting (page 39)
2. General Ice-Breakers (Appendix 8)
3. Listening Skills Material (Appendix 26)
4. Data Sheet on Baptism (Appendix 10)
5. Summary of Doctrinal Updates (Appendix 9)
6. The Sign of the Cross (Appendix 15)
7. Saints for Boys and Girls (Appendix 18)
8. "If Men Got Pregnant . . ." (Appendix 17)
9. "If Children . . ." (Appendix 20)
10. Evaluation Forms (6 per packet) (Appendix 22)

Appendix 6

CONTENTS OF PACKET FOR PARENTS

The welcome packet comes in an envelope with a picture of St. Gerard Majella (patron of our parish) and a place for the child's name.

Outside the Envelope
1. Cover Letter to Sponsors (Appendix 11)

Inside the Envelope
2. Welcome Letter to Couples with New Babies (Appendix 12)
3. Outline of the Baptism Process (Appendix 13)
4. Baptismal Registration Card
5. Donation Envelope (with explanation inside)
6. "If Children . . ." (Appendix 4)
7. The Sign of the Cross (Appendix 15)
8. Picture and Biography of St. Gerard Majella (patron of our parish)
9. Sample Parish Bulletin
10. "If Men Got Pregnant . . ." (Appendix 17)
11. Parish Skills Survey (Appendix 16)
12. "Babies Learn Sounds of Language by 6 Months" (Appendix 21)
13. Parents' Prayer after Their Child's Baptism (Appendix 20)

Appendix 7

CONTENTS OF PACKET FOR DIRECTOR/FACILITATOR

1. Formation Packet for Sponsors
2. Welcome Packet for Parents
3. Outline for an Information Night
4. Outlines for Three Sponsor Formation Sessions
5. General Letter to Prospective Baptism Sponsors
6. Specific Letter to Prospective Baptism Sponsors
7. Sample Homily on Baptismal Program
8. How We Envision:
   The Welcoming
   The Gathering
   The Celebration
   The Reflecting

Appendix 8

ICE BREAKER QUESTIONS FOR THE WELCOMING SESSION OR "HOME VISIT"

Since many adults may not have been practicing their faith, these ice breaker questions focus on the child. This enables the parents to "ease into" what might be a new and potentially uncomfortable situation.

1. How did you feel when you found out you were expecting a child?

2. How has the baby changed other relationships in your house? In your family?

3. Have you already selected the godparents? If so, how did you go about it?

4. How has your life changed now that there's a new addition?

5. What are your hopes for the baby?

6. What are you *most* willing to do for your baby?

7. What story would you *most* love to tell your baby?

8. What is the best quality you see in your baby?

9. What do you want your baby to *see* in this life?

10. What has your baby taught you about God so far?

11. Name some of the games you will play with your baby.

12. What did you think or feel when your mother or father or other important adult held your baby for the first time?

13. How did you feel the first day home with your baby?

14. What was it like when you first felt the baby move?

15. How did it feel when you first called your baby by his or her name?

16. How did you come to choose your child's name? Is there anyone else in the family with that name?

17. Tell us about some of the advice you've received from other people regarding the raising of your child.

18. Are there any traditions in your family concerning baptism, like:
- how soon the baptism should take place?
- who the godparents should be?
- what the baby should wear?
- who takes care of the party details?
- what presents your baby has received or should receive?

19. Describe some of the dreams you have for your child?

20. What are some adjustments you've already had to make for your baby?

Appendix 8

Appendix 9

SUMMARY OF DOCTRINAL UPDATES

- There is only one world and it belongs to God.
- Persons are whole and entire graced creatures, not pieces and parts.
- Christ's presence is alive in ten thousand places (Gerard M. Hopkins).
- With Paul, we believe that all persons are united in Christ Jesus.
- What we do as Christians is to seek out and name God's goodness.

- Baptism is a way of being connected to God and the community.
- Through baptism we affirm our faith at the font while en route to the feast.
- The old definitions of sacraments were good but inadequate.
- Church membership is a personal and communal experience, not a private one.

- Baptism is the Christian community's response to live God's life always.
- People become church members when anointed with the oil of catechumens.
- Christ is the sacrament of God, the encounter point with God in time.
- Encounters with Christ lead to a process of conversion and transformation.
- This process begins by God's grace, and it continues with God and us together.

- For those with eyes of faith, God's life flows everywhere in the universe.
- There are natural, logical, and spiritual reasons for celebrating God-life.

- Recall experiences in everyday life that remind you of God's presence.
- How we see sacraments is rooted in how we see God in us and in the world.
- All sacraments move us from celebration to service of others.

- Grace is a love relationship with God, a relationship freely given, one which we cannot earn.
- Sacraments are not seven faucets of grace we can turn on and off at will.
- How God works through sacraments is often in the background, like "Muzak."
- Before, we tried to explain how some unbaptized persons were also saved.
- Limbo was an attempt to explain the fate of innocent unbaptized babies.
- Today we believe that God works in different ways in different persons.
- We celebrate what God does in us by means of public, communal, and ritual events.

- The word "sin" in the term "original sin" is problematic in itself.
- Obviously an infant or baby does not commit sin as we define it.
- The original condition: Paradise, lost by Adam's disobedient choice.
- Adam wanted it "all"; being a creature means not having it all.

- We recognize that infants are subject to the Evil One's influence.
- To deny the presence or power of the Evil One is foolishness.
- Removing original sin is hoping to restore creation to its original purity.
- An exorcism prayer at baptism asserts God's supreme power.

Appendix 9

Appendix 10

DATA SHEET ON BAPTISM
---

1. Godparents
- Only *one* godparent is necessary, and this person must be Roman Catholic;
  - If two godparents are desired:
    - one must be male and one must be female;
    - one must be **Roman Catholic**, the other must be a **baptized Christian**.
- Non-Christians, because they do not believe in Jesus as their Lord and Savior, are not eligible to be godparents at baptisms in a Catholic church.
- Qualifications: godparents must have received the eucharist and have been confirmed; and they must intend to support the child in the practice of the Catholic faith.

2. What's in a Name: Choosing One
- First, see the list of names provided in Appendix 18.
- Second, it is *recommended* that the child's first or middle name or both be related to a saint's name, but this is *not* required.
- However, the name cannot be anti-Christian or signal a rejection of Christianity, as occurred when basketball star Lew Alcindor became a Muslim and changed his name to Kareem Abdul-Jabaar.

3. What if the Baby Has Already Been Baptized?
- We respect this fact; it happens because of genuine need, at the suggestion of medical personnel soon after birth or prior to surgery, at the insistence of parents, and sometimes through the unsolicited action of a doting relative.
- Simply mark the facts on the registration card: which hospital or where it took place, and when and under what circumstances. Our secretary will take care of the rest.
- While we won't be pouring the water again, we will supply the ceremonies that were omitted in the emergency situation: for example, the pre-baptismal

anointing will occur in the *gathering*, the post-baptismal anointing in the *baptismal* celebration, and the giving of the candle during the *reflection* follow-up session.

4. What if the parents aren't married?

- The Church began years ago to address this situation. We also now recognize that there are numerous reasons why the parents may not be married. We do not refuse to baptize an infant simply because the child lacks the support of two parents married to one another. The important dimension is that one parent is ready and willing to promise to raise the child in the Catholic faith.
- Obviously this and other situations require understanding and prudence. Our task, remember, is hospitality.

5. What if the parents are in a marriage that is not recognized by the Catholic Church?

- Make a note of this on the registration card where it says "Church of Marriage." Put whatever is appropriate, such as Justice of the Peace, civil marriage, Town Hall. It might also be another Christian church, a catering hall, a backyard, or the like.

6. What if the parents mention a divorce, one or more previous marriages, or that they are in the process of adopting the child?

- Please make a clear notation on the card, and we'll do the follow-up on it. You can also feel free to put them in touch with us, and we'll carry on any necessary discussion with them.

7. Which questions should we answer, and which should we refer back to the parish staff?

- Feel free to answer information questions, such as: the number of sessions; where each will be held; that we will all be there together for all the sessions; that you're glad to be with them and to introduce them to others in the parish community.
- You can always say "I don't know" or "I'll check this for you" or "That's something (a member of the parish staff) will help you with."

8. What if the child is no longer an infant?

- We can baptize children up to about five years of age as an infant. After that, we interview the *child and parents*. There is now a special process for young people approaching the age of reason, one which respects that a thinking human person is developing, one

Appendix 10

which will connect him or her to the wider Christian community through classes, rites, and a sponsor.

9. What if, during our discussions, it appears that the parents want to have their baby baptized for such reasons as: "It's a family tradition" or "My mother will disown us if I don't do it" or "I want to give my child something" and the like?

- The basic principle is that we have to get people *in* before we can welcome them and pray with them and share our faith and Jesus experiences with them. Our task is always to plant positive seeds, and not worry about the harvest or how these seeds will turn out.

10. What if someone wants a private ceremony or objects to coming to our sessions?

- Remember, *listening skills* always come first. There may be some real reasons why someone is struggling. Refer each case to us.

11. What if conflict develops between a parish sponsor and a parent?

- We live in an unfinished and imperfect world, so this reality can happen. Let us know and we'll speak with you about an adjustment or possibly another assignment. With your help, we will expand this question sheet during our follow-up sessions. Thanks for saying "Yes!" to this ministry.

Appendix 10

Appendix 11

WELCOME PACKET COVER LETTER TO SPONSORS

Dear Parish Sponsors:

This is a simple outline and reminder of the tasks you will accomplish upon *welcoming* and visiting the couple in their home:

- Greet and welcome them with the love and affection of Jesus himself. In this way the parents can see Jesus more clearly through you.

- Listen to them; they may have wonderful stories of the ways in which God brought them together, has worked in their lives, and has given them the power to share that love in the life of their child.

- Answer any factual questions you can concerning the baptismal program and its purpose. As we said in the formation sessions, you do not have to know every answer.

- Record the information on the baptism record card. We have hand-added two items:
    - the date of your interview with the couple;
    - the date and time of the gathering session they plan to attend.

Naturally we need to know the date of baptism and the specific Mass they are aiming for, too.

- Show the parents how to bless their baby, and encourage them to do so each day. Before you leave their house say with them the prayer found in the welcome packet. (A copy is printed below for you.)

- If you'd like to add the Our Father and make the sign of the cross on yourselves as an ending to your time together, feel free to do so.

- Be sure to get back to (name of person) here at the rectory right away, so we can track how many babies will be baptized at each specific Mass.

- It's crucial that you bring the record card to the gathering session on (date and time) and give it to the person facilitating the process that day.

- "Rejoice! It is the Lord in you who works to bring life."

A Parent's Prayer for Blessing a Baby

Loving God, Source of Life,
the gift of N. is precious and wonderful.
Thank you for entrusting us with this gift.
Open our eyes to see our union in your creative
 power,
and help us never to take this child for granted.

Thank you also for the power to bless N.
As we make the sign of the cross on this child,
we know that Jesus calls me to grow in his love.
Give us the patience to share Jesus' peace in our
 home,
and help us to guide N. day by day.
Amen.

Appendix 11

Appendix 12

WELCOME LETTER TO COUPLES WITH NEW BABIES

Congratulations on your newest addition, a gift from God. We rejoice with you in deciding to present your child for baptism into our parish community.

Because baptism is the first sacrament that initiates us into the church, we believe that spending quality time reflecting on our life experience, our relationship with God, and on how this child will alter them, can be a valuable investment for both the present and the future.

Enclosed in this packet is an outline of our process for greeting and guiding new young members into our Catholic faith community. We begin with YOU as parents in your home setting because, as the church continues to teach, you are the primary religious educators of your child. As your pastoral staff, we are ready to assist you in that sacred and wonderful duty. Please read carefully the information contained in this packet.

We hope that you will begin and end each day by blessing your child with the sign of the cross on her or his forehead. Even before baptism, this precious treasure God has sent you to nourish deserves the best possible care. This daily link between yourself and your child may even be an opportunity to strengthen your own faith in God's love for us.

May God bless you and give you the strength to do what Jesus did: to grow in wisdom, age, and grace before God and the world.

A Parents' Prayer for Blessing a Baby

Loving God, Source of life,
the gift of N. is precious and wonderful.
Thank you for entrusting us with this gift.
Open our eyes to see our union in your creative
    power,
and help us never to take this child for granted.

Thank you also for the power to bless N.
As we make the sign of the cross on this child,
We know that Jesus calls us to grow in his love.
Give us the patience to share Jesus' peace in our
    home,
and help us to guide N. day by day.
Amen.

Appendix 13

OUTLINE OF THE PROCESS FOR WELCOMING NEW INFANTS

Some parishes advise parents to come for baptismal preparation during pregnancy time. But we believe that your child should be present for *all four* experiences connected with his or her baptism, because the child is the reason we are getting to know one another better. There is also a short prayer service and liturgical symbol connected with each of these four stages. Each session focuses on the relationship you and your child enjoy as persons blessed by God.

The Welcoming Experience
happens at your home. It is an opportunity for some faithful members of our parish to greet you and obtain some basic registration information from you in preparation for your child's baptism. Our parish repressentatives will also leave some materials for you: these will include the invitation to make the sign of the cross on your child at least once a day from now on.

The Gathering Experience
occurs at the church (address and specific location) on (indicate day and time). A member of our parish staff will conduct a session which will help you to reflect more deeply on how active God has been by blessing your family with a new life. We will have some input and discussion on the changes which have occurred since your child's arrival. We conclude with the opening prayers of the baptismal ceremony, specifically, the first anointing with oil.

The Celebrating Experience
occurs on (indicate days and times). Your child deserves the very best when it comes to God's love, and we express that primary care when we gather at the eucharist. In the presence of a faithful and praying community and immediately after the homily, we will renew and profess our faith; then your child will be baptized by water and God's Holy Spirit. After the child receives the second anointing with oil (sacred chrism),

we will continue with the eucharist. The community will greet and congratulate you with love (specify location) after Mass.

The Reflecting Experience
will occur on (indicate date and time), usually a week after your child has been publicly welcomed into the parish community by his or her baptism. This session concentrates on naming the experiences, and on understanding more deeply, the symbols associated with baptism, including water, the cross, and the oil. Questions like "what pleases you about your child?" and "how does your child help you to ponder the mystery of God's love?" will be explored. The session will conclude with the lighting of a baptismal candle for each child and a blessing prayer for parents. An invitation to join with other couples in a small faith community will also be offered and explained.

REFLECTING

"This is my beloved child in whom I am well pleased"
(Mt 3:17).

Appendix 13

Appendix 14

"If Children . . ."

If children live with criticism,
    they learn to condemn.

If children live with hostility,
    they learn to fight.

If children live with ridicule,
    they learn to be shy.

If children live with tolerance,
    they learn to be patient.

If children live with encouragement,
    they learn confidence.

If children live with praise,
    they learn to apprciate.

If children live with fairness,
    they learn justice.

If children live with security,
    they learn to have faith.

If children live with approval,
    they learn to like themselves.

If children live with acceptance and friendship,
    they learn to find love in the world.

—Anonymous

Appendix 15

THE SIGN OF THE CROSS

When we cross ourselves, let it be with a real sign of the cross. Instead of using a small cramped gesture that gives no notion of its meaning, let us make a large unhurried sign, from forehead to breast, from shoulder to shoulder, consciously feeling how it includes the whole of us, our thoughts, our attitudes, our body and soul, every part of us at once, how it consecrates and sanctifies us.

It does so because it is the sign of the universe and the sign of our redemption. On the cross Christ redeemed mankind. By the cross he sanctifies mankind . . . We make the sign of the cross before we pray to collect and compose ourselves and to fix our minds and hearts and wills upon God. We make it when we finish praying in order that we may hold fast the gift we have received from God. In temptation we sign ourselves to be strengthened; in dangers, to be protected. The cross is signed upon us in blessings in order that the fulness of God's life may flow into the soul and fructify and sanctify us wholly.

Think of these things when you make the sign of the cross. It is the holiest of all signs. Make a large cross, taking time, thinking what you do. Let it take in your whole being,—body, soul, mind, will, thoughts, feelings, your doing and not doing,—and by signing it with the cross strengthen and consecrate the whole in the strength of Christ, in the name of the triune God.

Romano Guardini, *Sacred Signs*.
Reprinted with permission.

Appendix 16

PARISH SKILLS SURVEY

Our parish family includes people with a wide diversity of skills and experience. Many parishioners have indicated that they'd like to help with something, but don't know what's needed or whom to contact. Likewise, many parish projects never reach completion due to a lack of volunteers.

Be assured that throughout the year YOUR HELP IS NEEDED—for regular weekly activities, for annual events, and for numerous special projects.

Once you have completed this survey, your skills can be put on our computer, and can be easily accessed when needs arise. This is NOT a committment for any **specific** task.

Name: _____
Address: _____
Phone: (Home) _____
         (Business) _____

	Formal Training	Work Experience	General Knowledge
CONSTRUCTION			
Architecture	❑	❑	❑
General Contracting	❑	❑	❑
Carpentry	❑	❑	❑
Electrical	❑	❑	❑
HVAC	❑	❑	❑
Heating	❑	❑	❑
Plumbing	❑	❑	❑
Sheetrock/Spackling	❑	❑	❑
Painting	❑	❑	❑
Masonry	❑	❑	❑
Roofing	❑	❑	❑
Paving	❑	❑	❑
Concrete	❑	❑	❑
Lighting	❑	❑	❑
Detection & Alarm	❑	❑	❑
Doors/Windows	❑	❑	❑
Flooring/Carpeting	❑	❑	❑
Laborer	❑	❑	❑
Other (specify)	❑	❑	❑
LANDSCAPING	❑	❑	❑
SECURITY SERVICES	❑	❑	❑

HOUSEKEEPING SERVICES .. ❏ .... ❏ .... ❏
ADMINISTRATIVE
    Bookkeeping .... ❏ .... ❏ .... ❏
    Filing .... ❏ .... ❏ .... ❏
    Accounting .... ❏ .... ❏ .... ❏
    Typing/Wordprocessing .... ❏ .... ❏ .... ❏
    Computer Data Entry .... ❏ .... ❏ .... ❏
    Programming .... ❏ .... ❏ .... ❏
    Telemarketing .... ❏ .... ❏ .... ❏
    Other _____ ❏ .... ❏ .... ❏
INTERIOR DECORATING .... ❏ .... ❏ .... ❏
FLORAL DESIGN .... ❏ .... ❏ .... ❏
ARTS & CRAFTS .... ❏ .... ❏ .... ❏
HOME CARE SERVICES .... ❏ .... ❏ .... ❏
SOCIAL SERVICES .... ❏ .... ❏ .... ❏
FOOD PREPARATION .... ❏ .... ❏ .... ❏
YOUTH ACTIVITIES .... ❏ .... ❏ .... ❏
INSTRUCTION/TEACHING .... ❏ .... ❏ .... ❏
FOREIGN LANGUAGE (specify)
_____ ❏ .... ❏ .... ❏
OTHER SKILLS (specify)
_____ ❏ .... ❏ .... ❏
_____ ❏ .... ❏ .... ❏

    We would also like to identify those who may not have one of these unique skills but who have been blessed with the special gifts of giving and who are willing to donate their time and energies to assisting the parish in any capacity. If you are one of these very special people, please check the following box, ❏.

    Often materials and services not achieved through donations and volunteered time must be purchased. If you would like your company to be considered for such purchases, please provide the following information:

Company Name: _____
Phone: _____
Description of Services/Products: _____
_____
_____
_____

All information will be kept confidential.

Appendix 16

Appendix 17

"If Men Got Pregnant"

- Maternity leave would last two years . . . with full pay.
- There'd be a cure for stretch marks.
- Natural childbirth would become obsolete.
- Morning sickness would rank as the nation's number one health problem.
- All methods of birth control would be improved to 100 percent effectiveness.
- Children would be kept in the hospital until they were toilet trained.
- Men would be *eager* to talk about commitment.
- They wouldn't think twins were quite so cute.
- Fathers would demand that their *sons* be home from dates by 10:30 P.M.
- Men could use *their* briefcases as diaper bags.
- They'd have to stop saying, "I'm afraid I'll drop him."
- Paternity suits would be a line of clothes.
- Men would stay in bed for the entire nine months.
- Menus at most restaurants would list ice cream and pickles as an entrée.
- Women would rule the world.

—John Owens and Demetria Mudar

Appendix 18

SAINTS FOR BOYS AND GIRLS

Saints for Boys

Aaron:
Abraham: Abram
Adam: Adan
Adrian: Adrien, Hadrian
Alan: Alain, Allan, Allen
Alban: Alben, Albin, Alva
Albert: Adalbert, Alberto, Albrecht, Bert, Delbert
Alcuin:
Alexander: Alistair, Alec, Alex, Alejandro, Sacha, Sandor
Alexix: Alex, Alexei, Sasha
Aloysius:
Alphonse: Alfonso, Alonzo, Lon
Ambrose:
Amos:
Andrew: André, Andreas, Andres, Drew
Angelo: Angel
Anselm: Ansel
Anthony: Antoine, Anton, Antonio, Antony
Arnold: Arnaldo, Arnoldo
Augustine: Agostino, August, Augustin, Austin

Barnabas: Barnaby
Batholomew: Bart, Bartel, Bartolommeo, Barry
Basil: Vasily, Vassily
Bede:
Benedict: Benoit, Bennett, Benito
Benjamin: Benson
Bernard: Barnard, Bernadino, Bernardo, Bernhard, Nardo
Blase: Blaise
Bonaventure:
Boniface:
Brendan: Brandon, Brennan
Brian: Bryan, Bryant
Brice: Bruce
Bruno:

Camillus: Camille, Camillo
Casimir: Cass, Casper
Chad:
Charles: Carl, Carlo, Carlos, Carroll, Cary, Karl, Karol
Christian:
Christopher: Christophe, Cristobal, Cristoforo
Clair: Clare, Clarus
Clarence:
Claude: Claudius
Clement:

Saints for Boys

Colman:	
Columba:	
Constantine:	
Cormac:	
Cornelius:	Connor, Conor, Cornel, Neal, Neil
Cyril:	Cyr, Kyril
Damian:	Damiano, Damien, Damon
Daniel:	Dan, Niel
David:	
Denis:	Dennis, Dion, Dionysius, Sidney, Sydney
Dominic:	Domenico, Domingo, Dominick
Donald:	Don, Donal
Edmund	Edmond, Eamon, Ned
Edward:	Edoardo, Edouard, Eduard, Eduardo, Ned
Edwin:	
Elias:	Elijah
Emil:	Emile, Emilian, Emilion, Emilius, Emlyn
Emmanuel:	Emanuel, Immanuel, Manolo, Manuel
Eric:	Erik, Erich
Ernest:	Ernesto
Eugene:	Eugenio, Yevgeny
Eustace:	
Fabian:	
Felix:	Felician, Felicio
Ferdinand:	Fernando, Ferde, Fernand, Fernando
Fidelis:	Fidel
Francis:	Francesco, Francisco, Franco, Francois, Frank, Franz
Frederick:	Federico, Fred, Frederic, Friedrich
Gabriel:	
George:	
Gerald:	Geraldo, Garcia, Jerold
Gerard:	Gerhard, Gerado, Girado, Girard
Gervais:	Gervas, Gervase, Gervasius, Jarvis, Jervis
Gilbert	
Godfrey:	Geoffrey, Goffredo, Gottfried, Jeff, Jeffrey
Gregory:	Gregor, Gregoire, Gregorio
Guy:	Guido
Harold	
Harvey:	Hervé
Henry:	Emeric, Enrico, Harry, Heinrich, Henri, Rico
Herbert:	
Herman:	Armand, Armando, Ernan, Germain, German, Hermann, Hermé, Hernando
Hilarion:	Hilaire, Hilary
Hubert:	Umberto
Hugh:	Hughes, Hugo, Ugo
Ignatius:	Ignace, Ignacio, Ignazio, Inigo, Nacho
Isaac:	
Isidore:	Dore, Dorian
Ives:	Ivar, Iver, Ivo, Ivor, Yves
James:	Diego, Iago, Cacob, Jacques, Jaime, Santiago, Seamus, Shamus, Yakov

Appendix 18

Saints for Boys

Jeremias:	Geremia, Jeremy, Jeremiah
Jerome:	Geronimo, Hieronymus
Joachim:	Joaquin
Joel:	
John:	Baptiste, Evan, Gean, Giovanni, Hans, Ian, Ivan, Jan, Hohann, Hohannes, Jon, Uan, Sean, Shane, Shaun
Joseph:	Guiseppe, José, Josef
Jude:	
Julius:	Giles, Guilio, Jules, Julean, Julio
Justin	
Kenneth:	Canice, Kent
Kevin:	
Kieran:	
Killian:	Kilian
Ladislas:	Ladislaus, Lance, Lancelot, Lazlo, Vladislas
Lawrence:	Lars, Lauren, Laurence, Laurenz, Lauritz, Loren, Lorenzo
Leo:	Lee, Lon, Leov, Lionel
Leonard:	Leon, Leonardo, Leonhard
Leopold:	Leopoldo
Louis:	Alois, Aloysius, Lewis, Ludovico, Ludwig, Luigi, Luis
Luke:	Luc, Luca, Lucas, Lucian, Luciano, Lucio, Lucius
Malachy:	Malachi
Mark:	Marc, Marcel, Marco, Marcus, Markus
Martin:	Martino
Matthew:	Matt, Matteo, Matthaus, Matthias
Maurice:	Maur, Mauricio, Maurizio, Moritz, Morris
Maximilian:	Max, Massimiliano, Maxim
Meinrad:	Maynard
Mel:	
Michael:	Michel, Michele, Miguel, Mikhail, Mitchell
Moses:	
Nathaniel:	Nathanall
Nicholas:	Claus, Colin, Klaus, Nicol, Nicolo, Nikolaus, Niles, Nils
Noel:	
Norbert:	
Oliver:	
Otto:	Odo, Doilo
Owen:	
Pascal:	Paschal, Pasquale
Patrick:	Padraic, Patrice, Patricio, Patriztus
Paul:	Pablo, Paolo, Paulinus, Paulo, Powel
Peter:	Pedro, Perrin, Petrus, Pierce, Pierre, Piers, Pietro, Piotr
Philip:	Felipe, Filippo, Phelps, Philipp, Philippe, Philippus
Pius:	Pio
Quentin:	Quin, Quinn, Quintus
Ralph:	Rafe, Rafello, Raoul, Raul, Rolfe, Rodolfo, Rudolf, Rudolph, Rodolphus

Appendix 18

Saints for Boys

Raphael:	Rafael, Rafaelle, Raffaello
Raymond:	Raimondo, Ramon, Raymund, Redmond
Reginald:	Reinhold, Reinwald, Reynold, Rinaldo, Ronald
René:	Renato, Renatus
Richard:	Ricardo, Riccardo
Robert:	Roberto, Robin, Rupert, Ruprecht
Roderic:	Roderick, Roderico, Rodrigo, Rory, Rurik
Roger:	Hodge, Rogelio, Rory, Rudiger, Ruggero
Romanus:	Romain, Roman, Romano, Romaric, Romeo
Ronald:	Ronaldo, Aldo
Rudolph:	Rolfe, Rodofo, Rodolphus, Rudolf
Rupert:	Robert, Ruprecht
Salvatore:	Salvador, Salvator
Samuel:	Samuele
Sebastian:	
Sigmund:	Siegmund, Sigismondo, Sigismund
Simon:	Simeon, Simone
Stanislaus:	Stanislao, Stanislas, Stanley
Stephen:	Esteban, Stefan, Stefano, Stefen, Stephan, Steven, Sven
Terence:	Terrence, Terry
Thaddeus:	
Theodore:	Feodor, Tad, Teodore, Theo, Theodotius
Thomas:	Tomas, Tommaso
Timothy:	Timoteo, Timotheus
Titus:	Tito
Tobias:	Tobia, Tobiah, Tobit
Urban:	Urbano, Urbanus
Valerius:	Valentin, Valens, Valentine, Valentino, Valentinus, Valerian, Valeriano, Valerio
Victor:	Victorio, Vittorio
Vincent:	Vincente, Vincentius, Vincenzo
Vladimir:	
Walter:	Gualthieri, Walther
Wenceslaus:	Vinceslao, Wencelas
Wilfrid:	
William:	Guiglielmo, Guiliermo, Guillaume, Wilhelm, Willis
Xavier:	
Zachary:	Zaccaria, Zacharias, Zechariah

Saints for Girls

Abigail:	Abbie, Abby, Gail, Gale
Ada:	Adalberta
Adele:	Adalie, Adela, Adelaide, Adelheid, Adelina, Adeline, Aline, Della
Adria:	Adriana, Adrienne
Agatha:	Agathe, Agathy
Agnes:	Agnella, Agnete, Agnita, Ines, Inez, Neysa, Nina, Ninette, Rachel

Appendix 18

Saints for Girls

Albina:	Alba, Bianca, Blanche
Alberta:	Albertina (*Fem. of* Albert)
Alessandra:	Aleth, Alex, Alexandra, Alexandrina, Alexis, Cassandra, Sandra (*Fem. of* Alexander)
Alice:	Aleydis, Alicia, Alisa, Alison, Alix, Alyce, Alys, Elissa, Else, Ilsa, Illse
Alma:	
Amanda:	(*Fem. of* Amandus)
Amata:	Amy, Aimee (*Fem. of* Amatius)
Anastasia:	Stacey, Stasia, Stathia, Statia
Andrea:	(*Fem. of Andrew*)
Angela:	Angel, Angelica, Angelina, Angelique, Angelita
Ann:	Anita, Anna, Annabel, Anne, Annabella, Annette, Hannah, Nan, Nancy, Nanette, Ninon
Antonia:	Antoinette, Antonia, Tanya, Toni, Tonica (*Fem. of* Anthony)
Audrey:	(See Etheldra)
Barbara:	
Beatrice:	Beatrix, Beatriz
Bernadette:	Bernardine, Bernice, Nadine (*Fem. of* Bernard)
Bertha:	Berta, Bertild, Bertilla
Brenda:	(*Fem. of* Brendan)
Bridget:	Birgit, Bride, Bridey, Bridig, Brigid, Brigida, Brigit, Brigitta, Brigitte
Camille:	Camelia, Camilla (*Fem. of* Camillus)
Carmel:	Carmelita, Carnella
Carol:	Arlene, Arlette, Carey, Carla, Carole, Carola, Caroline, Carolyn, Charlene, Charlotte, Cheryl (*Fem. of* Charles)
Catherine:	Catalina, Caterina, Karen, Kate, Kateri, Katherine, Kathleen, Mathryn, Katrina, Kay, Kit, Kitty, Tina
Cecelia:	Caecilia, Cecile, Cecily, Ceil, Cicely, Cicly, Sheila
Chantale:	
Charity:	Cara
Christina:	Christian, Christine, Kirsten, Iirsten, Kristin, Nina, Tina (*Fem. of* Christ)
Clare:	Chiara, Claire, Clairette, Clara, Clareta, Clarice, Clarissa, Carita
Claudia:	Claudette, Claudine (*Fem. of Claude*)
Clementine:	Clemence, Clementia, Clementina, Klementine (*Fem. of* Clement)
Colette:	Coleen, Colleen (*Fem. of* Nicholas)
Columbine:	Colombina, Columba, Columbia, Columbina (*Fem. of* Columban) or St. Colette
Conception:	Concepcion, Concepta
Constance:	Constantia, Constanza, Constanze (*Fem. of* Constantine)
Consuela:	Consolata, Consuelo
Cornelia:	Cora (*Fem. of* Cornelius)
Cynthia:	(*Fem. of Synesius*)
Daniela:	*Danielle, Danette* (Fem. of Daniel)
Daria:	Darlene
Deborah:	Debora, Debra

Appendix 18

Saints for Girls

Denise:	(*Fem. of* Denis)
Diana:	Cynthia, Diane, Dinah
Dolores:	Dolor, Dolorita, Lola, Lolita
Dominica:	Dominga, Dominique (*Fem. of* Dominic)
Domitilla:	(*Fem. of* Domitian)
Donata:	Dona, Donna, Donatilla
Doris:	Dora, Doreen (*Fem. of* Theodore)
Dorothy:	Dorothea, Dorotea (*Fem. of* Theodore)
Edith:	Eadie, Eda, Edythe
Edwina:	Edna (*Fem. of* Edwin)
Eleanor:	Elenord, Eleonore, Elinor, Leanore, Lee, Lenora, Lenore, Leora, Nell, Nellie, Nelly
Elizabeth:	Alise, Aliza, Babette, Bella, Belle, Bess, Bessie, Beth, Betsy, Bette, Betty, Elisa, Elise, Eliza, Elsa, Else, Elsie, Isabel, Isabella, Isobel, Lee, Lilian, Lisa, Lisabeth, Lisbeth, Lise, Lisette, Lison
Emily:	Amelia, Emelie, Emeline, Emilia, Emiliana, Emma (*Fem. of* Emil) or St. Emma
Enrica:	Henrietta (*Fem. of* Henry)
Erica:	*Erika* (Fem. of Eric)
Ernestine:	(*Fem. of* Ernest)
Esperanza:	
Esther:	Edissa, Vanessa
Etheldra:	Audrey, Ethel, Etheldreda, Ethlreda
Eugenia:	Eugenie, Gina (*Fem. of* Eugene)
Eulalia:	Eulalie
Eunice:	
Eve:	Eva, Eveline, Evelyn, Evita
Fabiola:	
Faith:	Fay, Fe, Fidelia
Felicity:	Felicia, Felice, Felicienne, Felicita, Felicitos
Felipa:	(*Fem. of* Philip)
Florence:	Fleur, Flora, Florentia, Florentina
Frances:	Cesca, Fanchon, Fanny, Fenna, France, Francesca, Franchetti, Francine, Francois, Frannie (*Fem. of* Francis) or St. Frances
Freda:	Alfreda, Alfrida, Althryda
Frederica:	Frederika (*Fem. of* Frederic)
Gabriela:	Gabriella, Gabrielle, Briel (*Fem. of* Gabriel)
Gemma:	
Genevieve:	Ginette, Violane, Yolanda, Blanche
Georgia:	Georgianna, Georgana, Georgette (*Fem. of* George)
Geraldine:	Geralda, Geralyn (*Fem. of* Gerald)
Germaine:	
Gertrude:	Gerda, Trudy
Gladys:	
Gloria:	
Grace:	
Guadalupe:	Lupe
Gwen:	Gwendoline
Harriet:	Hally, Hariette, Harriette, Henrietta, Henriette (*Fem. of* Henry)

Appendix 18

Saints for Girls

Helen:	Aileen, Alene, Aline, Celine, Eileen, Elain, Elaine, Elane, Eleanore, Elena, Ella, Ellen, Helena, Helene, Ilone, Len, Lenore, Nell, Nellie, Selina, Seline
Hilda:	Hildegard
Hope:	
Ida:	
Ignatia:	(*Fem. of* Ignatius)
Immaculata:	
Irene:	Irena, Renata, Renée
Irma:	Erma, Irmina, Irmine
Jacqueline:	Jacoba
Jane:	Giovanna, Janet, Janice, Jean, Jeanette, Jeanine, Jeanne, Jessica, Jessie, Joan, Jo Ann, Joanna, Joanne, Johanna, Juana, Juanita, June, Nita (*Fem. of* John) or St. Jane or St. Joan
Jennifer:	(*Fem. of* Wilfred) or Jane or Genevieve
Josephine:	Guiseppina, Josefa, Josepha, Josette, Josianne, Yvette (*Fem. of* Joseph)
Judith:	Judy (*Fem. of Jude*)
Julia:	Jill, Juliana, Julianna, Julie, Juliet, Juliette
Justina:	Justa, Justine, Tina
Laura:	*Lara, Laraine, Laureen, Laurenta, Laurentia, Laurette, Loretta, Lorraine*
Leona:	Lee, Leonie, Leonita (*Fem. of* Leo)
Lilian:	Lila, Lily, Lillian (Blessed Virgin)
Louise:	Alison, Aloysia, Eloisa, Eloise, Heloise, Lois, Louisa, Luisa, Luise (*Fem. of* Louis) or St. Louise
Lucy:	Luc, Luce, Lucette, Lucia, Lucie, Lucien, Lucienne, Lucilla, Lucille, Lucina, Lucinda, Luz
Lydia:	
Mabel:	(Amabilis . . . Blessed Mother)
Magdalene:	Maddalena, Madeline, Magda, Marlene
Manuela:	(*Fem. of* Emmanuel)
Marcella:	Marcelina, Marcelle
Marcia:	Marsha (*Fem. of* Mark)
Margaret:	Greta, Gretchen, Madge, Maggie, Maisie, Margarita, Marge, Margery, Margo, Margot, Marguerite, Marina, Marjorie, Pearl, Pegeen, Peggy, Rita
Martha:	Marta, Marthe
Martina:	Martine
Mary:	Mae, Maime, Mara, Maria, Marian, Marianna, Maribel, Marie, Marietta, Mariette, Marigold, Marilyn, Marya, Maureen, May, Mirella, Miriam, Moira, Molly, Polly
Matilda:	Mathilde, Maud, Maude, Tilda, Tillie
Maura:	
Melanie:	Melania, Melinda
Mercedes:	Merced, Mercy (Blessed Mother)
Michaela:	Micaela, Michaeleen, Michelle (*Fem. of* Michel)
Mildred:	Melissa, Millie, Milly
Monica:	Mona, Monique
Myra:	(*Fem. of* Myron)
Nadine:	Nadia
Natalie:	Matalia, Natasha, Nathalie

Appendix 18

Saints for Girls

Name	Variants
Nicole:	Nicola, Nicolette (*Fem. of* Nicholas)
Nora:	Honora, Honorée, Norah, Noreen, Norine (St. Honorata)
Olga:	
Olive:	Oliva, Olivia
Patricia:	(*Fem. of* Patrick)
Paula:	Paulette, Pauline (*Fem. of* Paul)
Priscilla:	
Rafaela:	(*Fem. of* Raphael)
Ramona:	Mona, Raimunda (*Fem. of* Raymond)
Rebecca:	
Regina:	Reine, Renee (Blessed Mother)
Rita:	
Roberta:	(*Fem. of* Robert)
Rosaria:	(Blessed Mother)
Rose:	Rosa, Rosalie, Rosiland, Rosalinda, Rosaline, Rosalyn, Roseanna, Rosemarie, Rosemonde, Rosetta
Ruth:	
Sabina:	Savina
Sandra:	(*Fem. of* Alexander)
Sarah:	Sally, Sara, Sarai, Shari
Selma:	(*Fem. of* Anselm)
Serafina:	Fina, Seraphia, Seraphina
Sharon:	(Blessed Mother)
Silvia:	Sylva, Sylvaine, Sylvette, Sylvia, Sylvie
Simone:	Simona, Mona (*Fem. of* Simon)
Solange:	
Sophia:	Nadia, Nadine, Sofia, Sonia, Sonya, Sophie (Title of God) or St. Sophia
Stella:	Estella, Estelle, Estrella, Estrellita, (Blessed Mother)
Stephanie:	Esta, Estancia, Stefanie (*Fem. of* Stephen)
Susanna:	Susan, Suzanne, Suzette
Theodora:	Dolly, Dora, Dorothy, Theodosia
Theresa:	Teresa, Terese, Terry, Therese, Tracy
Thomasina:	Tomasa, Tomasina, Tomasine (*Fem. of* Thomas)
Trinidad	(Trinity)
Ursula:	
Valery:	Valeria, Valerie
Veronica:	Bernice, Vera, Veronique
Victoria:	
Cincentia:	Vincenza
Virginia:	(Blessed Mother)
Vivian:	(From Bibiana)
Wilhelmina:	(*Fem. of* William)
Winifred:	
Yvette:	Yvonne
Zita:	
Zoe:	

Appendix 18

Appendix 19

REMINDERS FOR BAPTISM

1. Come early with the baby: fifteen minutes before Mass is good. Give yourself plenty of time to be seated before the celebration. And yes, Mass will start on time.

2. Parents should sit toward the end of the pew, "on the aisle." One of the parents holds the baby from the beginning of Mass. Remember, parents take primary responsibility for their child in all things, including raising a child in the faith.

3. After the baptism itself, after the anointing with chrism and a short prayer that mentions the baby's white baptismal garment, relative and friends other than the parents are welcome to hold the baby.

We recommend that godparents, because of their important role, take turns providing this service.

4. The ushers may ask you or your relatives to bring up the gifts of bread and wine. This is an opportunity we offer people at every Mass in our parish, and it is a privilege.

5. Family photographers (as well as those using camcorders) are welcome at the baptism.

But ask them not to use flash, and to stay in their seats during the baptism itself. We request this so that everyone can focus on the important sacred action at the font.

6. Some babies need pacifiers or bottles during a baptismal Mass. Bring these if your baby needs them. But in order to avoid flying pacifiers, please take the pacifier out of the baby's mouth just before the baptism.

7. At the end of the Mass, we will ask parents and godparents with the newly-baptized *only* to join in the exit procession. This will allow the other members of the assembly to congratulate you and to personally ask God to bless your child.

8. Some parents have asked us about the duties of godparents. These duties are:
- to be persons of faith, believers in God and in God's church;

- to support parents in their duty as Christian mothers and fathers;
- to encourage the child spiritually for the rest of his or her life, especially by praying each day for that child;
- to be a good example in word and deed for the child.

May God bless and protect the child whose new life we celebrate in baptism. Amen! Amen! Amen!

Appendix 19

Appendix 20

PARENTS' PRAYER AFTER THEIR CHILD'S BAPTISM

Creator God,
we thank you for sharing your life-giving power with us.

We praise you
for the gift of N., our daughter/son,
whom we dedicated to you today.

Washed in the holy waters of baptism
and embraced as a member of our (name of parish) faith community,
N. is the flower of our love.

On this feast of her/his baptism into Christ Jesus and into Christ's church,
we are filled with wonder and joy.
For N. has a holy purpose in life:
as one of your children,
she/he is a royal and priestly person.

Loving God,
as N.'s parents we ask for your strength and support.

Be with us always
so that we may show her/him the path of life,
the holy way of Jesus Christ,
by the way we live your love
in loving one another, our neighbors, and ourselves.

We also ask, Gentle God,
that the parishioners of (name of parish)
will support us in prayer today and in the years to come.

Help us to encourage N. to become
the unique and creative person she/he is meant to be.

Bless us her/his parents, her/his godparents,
and all her/his future friends and Christian companions.

Help us all to be good examples for N. by living the virtues
of justice and peace, of truth and hope, of faithfulness and love.

Watch over our daughter/son all the days of her/his life.
As we bless her/him today, we promise to worship you always through Jesus our Brother and Savior. AMEN.

Appendix 21

BABIES LEARN SOUNDS OF LANGUAGE BY 6 MONTHS

by Sandra Blakeslee

Babies learn the basic sounds of their native language by the age of 6 months, long before they utter their first words, and earlier than researchers had thought, a new study suggests.

The findings indicate that recognition of these sounds is the first step in the comprehension of spoken language. As a result, the researchers suggest, babies whose hearing is damaged by chronic ear infections may have lifelong language problems, and the way parents speak to their infants exerts important influences on language learning.

Previous studies suggested that infants' sound perception changes by about 1 year old, when children begin to understand that sounds convey word meanings.

The new research, reported in the current issues of *Science*, was conducted by Dr. Patricia Kuhl of the University of Washington in Seattle and colleagues at Stockholm University in Sweden, the Massachusetts Institute of Technology and the University of Texas in Austin.

Adaptability of Newborn

Newborns are language universalists, Dr. Kuhl said. Able to learn any sound in any language, they can distinguish all the sounds that humans utter. But adults are language specialists, she said. Exposure to their native language reduces their ability to perceive speech sounds that are not in that native tongue. Thus Japanese infants can hear the difference between the English sounds "la" and "ra," but Japanese adults cannot because their language does not contrast those sounds.

Dr. Kuhl said she and her colleagues set out to discover when, during language development, experience alters sound perception and to explore the nature of the change. She said she had thought it could be earlier than other researchers believed.

Recognizing Slight Differences

To test her idea, she used the concept of phonetic prototypes: idealized mental representations of the key sounds in a given language. An English prototype sound is the vowel linguists write as "i," pronounced as in the word "fit." When an adult English speaker hears something very close to this "i" sound (as when the sound is spoken by someone with a head cold), Dr. Kuhl said, the listener will hear the prototype "i" and not the slight variation. The prototype sound acts like a magnet, she said, pulling all similar sounds into one mental slot for language processing.

But the same is not true of foreign languages. Because English speakers have not memorized the prototype of a foreign vowel—like the Swedish vowel "y" (an EE sound produced with front-rounded lips), they can discern when the vowel is pronounced slightly differently. They have no "magnet" that makes the sounds identical.

Using identical computer equipment to generate prototype Swedish and English sounds, Dr. Kuhl and her colleagues tested the magnet effect on 64 6-month-old babies in Sweden and the United States. During the experiment, each baby sat on its mother's lap and listened to pairs of "i" and "y" sounds. Babies were trained to look over their left shoulders when they heard a difference in the sounds (they would see a cut puppet bang a drum) and to ignore any sound pairs that seemed the same.

American babies routinely ignored the different pronunciations of "i" because they heard it as the same sound, Dr. Kuhl said. But they could distinguish slight variations in the "y" sounds.

The exact opposite was true of the Swedish babies, she said. They ignored the variations in "y" because they sounded the same, while they noticed the variations in "1."

The experiment confirms that linguistic experience in the first half year of life alters at infant's perception of speech sounds, Dr. Kuhl said. Infants show a significantly stronger magnet effect for their native language prototypes.

The study shows that phonetic perception does not depend on the emerging use of words, Dr. Kuhl said, and that language experience shapes perception far earlier than anyone expected.

Appendix 21

The research calls attention to the language tutoring role of parents, Dr. Kuhl said. By talking "motherese" with its high pitch, exaggerated intonation and clear pronunciation, she said, parents help babies acquire phonetic prototypes that are building blocks to language.

The study also underscores the importance of treating chronic ear infections in infants, Dr. Kuhl said. There is evidence that such infections may impair language development later in life.

■ ■ ■

Appendix 21

Appendix 22

PARENT EVALUATION SHEET

Please help us improve our program by completing this brief evaluation form.

1. This process was: (check one)
   ___ Excellent
   ___ Very good
   ___ Good
   ___ Not good

2. I would like to get involved in this program by becoming a parish sponsor:
   ___ Yes
   ___ No
   ___ Maybe. Here's my name and phone number:

   _____
   _____

* * * * *

Please tell us:

What you liked most about our baptismal program:

What you liked least about the program:

Other comments:

Your name (optional):

_____

THANK YOU.

Appendix 23

PARISH SPONSOR EVALUATION SHEET

1. Name anything you found ENJOYABLE about working in our baptism program.

Name anything you found DIFFICULT to do in our baptism program.

2. WE'RE LOOKING FOR QUOTABLE QUOTES, our version of rave reviews! Can you recall any comments from the parents, either ABOUT THEMSELVES or their CHILDREN, that would help demonstrate their satisfaction with our celebrations and program?

What STORY (or event or action) involving their child do you most clearly remember at this time?

3. THE GOOD, THE BAD AND THE UGLY!

    A. Recall the WELCOMING SESSION in the home. What's the BEST thing that came out of that session? Does anything need clarification?

    B. Recall the GATHERING SESSION on the SECOND SUNDAY at the church. What was the best part about that session? Is there anything that needs "tightening up" or clearing up?

C. Recall the BAPTISM at Mass: how did it go? Name anything you can suggest to help things run more smoothly.

D. Recall the FOLLOW-UP session. Name anything you liked about it, and tell us what you think needs fixing.

4. LIST ANY QUESTIONS OR ISSUES THAT CAME UP IN THIS PROCESS which we never spoke about during the training session, but ought to be included from now on. You may comment in any way you see fit.

5. Are you ready for a get-together session to share faith and some of your experiences with other sponsors?
 ____ Yes   ____ No   ____ Don't Know

Tell us your BEST DAY OF THE WEEK for a meeting:

Suggest what you believe is the BEST TIME:

We want you to know that we have received many COMPLIMENTS and AFFIRMATIONS of your labors of love. It is YOU who are working as partners with Jesus Christ, and empowering people with signs of His presence. Thank you for all you do, and for putting yourselves into this project with such enthusiasm!

Appendix 23

Appendix 24

REMINDER LETTER TO PARENTS OF THE NEWLY-BAPTIZED CHILD

Dear _____ :

    We have missed you these past months.
    We are sorry that you and your (daughter/son) (name of child in CAPS) were not able to be with us for our recent baptismal reflection session.
    This follow-up session includes a sharing of the experiences you and other parents had at the baptism of your child, as well as the reception of the baptismal candle, a special blessing for parents of recently baptized children, and an invitation to continue to be a regular member of our parish worshiping community.
    We hope that you will be able to join us for the session on (date, day, time, and location). I encourage you to contact your parish baptismal sponsor (telephone number) before that date, so that she/he/they can be with you at the reflection session you attend.
    Until we can again share God's love and the joy of your newest arrival, may the Lord Jesus bless you and your growing family with true wisdom and lasting peace.

Sincerely,

Appendix 25

INVITATION TO A REUNION MASS

Dear _____ :

Because the sacrament of baptism brought us together to welcome and celebrate your (son's/daughter's) (child's name) new life in Christ Jesus, we want to help you as a parent build on that good foundation.

As one way of keeping in mind that Jesus leads us always from the baptismal font to the banquet feast of eucharist, we invite you to a reunion Mass of all those whose children have been baptized over the last (period of time). It is scheduled for (date, day, time, location).

You might like to join the other families of recently baptized children who will be coming to this Mass. We have reserved a special section of the church for these parents and children, but, if you wish, feel free to sit wherever you like.

You can help us offer proper hospitality by calling (phone number) to let us know how many people will be attending. We will begin serving refreshments about ten minutes after the Mass.

Until we are together again for this special reunion, may the Lord Jesus bless and protect you and those whom God has entrusted you to love.

Sincerely,

P.S. As part of our pastoral outreach to you and others in our parish, we also want you to know of another service we offer. If you or someone you know is in a marital relationship that is not recognized as valid by the church, we are prepared to help rectify this situation. This issue can be particularly important to parents who desire to receive the eucharist with their children, but cannot do so at the moment because of their marriage status. We will sit down and explain the steps and procedures necessary to return a person to the church's full sacramental life. Please call (phone number) to make an appointment.

Appendix 25

Appendix 26
LISTENING SKILLS
Page 1

People I spend time with . . .	👂	♡	👄	☞	🔍

Appendix 26
LISTENING SKILLS

Page 2

Reflective Listening . . .

"Mirror, Mirror on the wall, who's the fairest of them all . . ."

Definition:

Reflective Listening is a two fold process which involves:

1. Reflecting the CONTENT of what the other person is saying in his or her words or body language.
2. Reflecting the FEELINGS of what the other person is saying in his or her words or body language.

Description:

Reflective Listening uses STATEMENTS only, and *no questions!*

e.g. #1 "You think that . . . . . ." (Reflects content of speaker)
e.g. #2 "You feel (are) . . . . . ." (Reflects feeling of speaker)

Delineation:

Reflective Listening happens in three kinds of responses

Following Skills:	Door Openers (You have a lot on your mind . . .)
	Acknowledgements (Uh-huh, Oh, Wow . . .)
	Active Silence (Focus on Speaker)
Responding Skills:	Paraphrasing (In other words you . . .)
	Reflecting Feelings (You are disappointed . . .)
	Reflecting Meanings (You are disappointed because you think . . .)
	Summarizing (All in all you think . . . and feel . . .)
Attending Skills:	The Body Language of Listening
	Eye Contact
	Posture— Facing speaker, inclined toward them, open position
	Gestures— Responsive, relaxed
	Environment— Privacy, no barriers

Listener   Speaker

Appendix 26
LISTENING SKILLS
Page 3

Taking Your Temperature

I'm okay

You're Okay

I'm Okay

You're NOT Okay

I   Other   I   Other

Skill-None!

Skill—
- Reflective Listening
  —To Content
  —To Feelings
    "Mad"
    "Sad"
    "Glad"
    "Scared"

Listening Log:

WHO:
(I "Listened" to)

FEELINGS:
(I "Heard")

RESPONSES:
(I Made)